Gienside Free Libr
215 South Keswick Avenue
Glenside, PA 19038-4420

W9-BMX-802

PRONUNCIATION EXERCISES IN

ENGLISH

PRONUNCIATION EXERCISES

in

ENGLISH

(Revised Edition)

**Including Drills for the Correction
of Faulty Accent and Intonation**

By
M. ELIZABETH CLAREY
and
ROBERT J. DIXSON

PRENTICE HALL REGENTS, Englewood Cliffs, NJ 07632

© 1947, 1963 by M. Elizabeth Clarey and R.J. Dixson Associates

 Published by Prentice-Hall, Inc.
A Division of Simon & Schuster
Englewood Cliffs, NJ 07632

All rights reserved. No part of this book may be
reproduced, in any form or by any means,
without permission in writing from the publisher.

Printed in the United States of America

10 9 8 7 6 5 4 3

ISBN 0-13-730854-X   01

Prentice-Hall International (UK) Limited, *London*
Prentice-Hall of Australia Pty. Limited, *Sydney*
Prentice-Hall Canada Inc., *Toronto*
Prentice-Hall Hispanoamericana, S.A., *Mexico*
Prentice-Hall of India Private Limited, *New Delhi*
Prentice-Hall of Japan, Inc., *Tokyo*
Simon & Schuster Asia Pte. Ltd., *Singapore*
Editora Prentice-Hall do Brasil, Ltda., *Rio de Janeiro*

CONTENTS

PREFACE: The Teaching of Pronunciation*

The teaching of English pronunciation is both a simple and a complicated procedure. It is simple in that such teaching involves merely the drilling of students on the various sounds of English. Those conscientious teachers who have good pronunciation can do this. They offer themselves as models of good pronunciation, correcting as best they can any errors which the students make.

Teachers should keep in mind at all times, of course, that ear training is extremely important in the teaching of any foreign language. Drill on the proper articulation of sounds is necessary, but ear training is even more fundamental. Students must hear a sound clearly before they can reproduce it. Concepts of quality, pitch, and volume originate in the hearing area of the brain. The tonal image is heard mentally before it is actually produced by the voice. If this image is not exact, the production of the sound will not be accurate. Consequently, all pronunciation drills should be continued over as long a period of time as possible. Teachers should never jump from one exercise to another but should continue working on each individual sound until the sound is heard clearly by the students, and the proper ear and hearing habits have been established.

On the other hand, although the teaching of pronunciation through mere imitation is an easy method to follow, such teaching can be, at the same time, a much more specialized task. If teachers are to do more than simply guide their students through the various sounds, they should first understand some of the basic principles of English speech production. They should also be able to make use of these principles in their teaching. In this case, the effectiveness of their teaching does not depend so much upon the teaching methods or techniques that they employ but rather

* The material which follows is derived almost entirely from Chapter VII, The Teaching of Pronunciation, of *Practical Guide to the Teaching of English as a Foreign Language*, by Robert J. Dixson.

upon their knowledge and understanding of the general subject matter.

In this introduction, we should like to discuss briefly some of the aspects of English speech which relate particularly to the correction of a foreign accent.

Phonetics—The International Phonetic Alphabet

Phonetics has been defined as the study of speech sounds and the art of pronunciation. Teachers who attempt to teach pronunciation automatically make some use of phonetics. Teachers' knowledge of theoretical phonetics may be very limited, but, in correcting the accent of their foreign students, they unconsciously make use of whatever they know. They guide their students toward correct pronunciation through frequent drill. They make a careful distinction between one sound and another. All of this is phonetics. A distinction should be made here, of course, between *phonetics* and *phonetic symbols*. These terms are not identical, although many people tend to use them indiscriminately. While phonetics is concerned with the study of speech sounds and proper pronunciation, phonetic symbols remain simply one of the tools which the phonetician uses in analyzing language. It is quite possible to teach pronunciation without making use of phonetic symbols. It is also possible to make extensive use of such symbols without succeeding in teaching pronunciation.

The most common set of phonetic symbols now in use are those which make up the alphabet of the International Phonetic Association. Most teachers of English as a foreign language are already familiar with this International Phonetic Alphabet (IPA). Phonetic symbols of this alphabet now appear, in greater or lesser degree, in most modern textbooks. The language teachers' problem, generally, is to determine the extent to which they should make use of these IPA symbols in their own teaching.

Some teachers make extensive use of phonetic symbols and find them very useful in their teaching. In some cases, the extent to which such symbols are used depends upon the particular class situation. In a well-organized school system where students begin to study English in the lower grades and continue the study of

English for several years, there is both time and opportunity to make phonetics an integral part of the program. In shorter, more intensive courses there is often little time left for phonetic transcriptions of any kind. Many teachers, moreover, are not sufficiently trained to use the IPA system efficiently. Students in some circumstances react unfavorably to learning any type of phonetic symbols.

The theory underlying the use of phonetic symbols is, of course, simple and logical. The International Phonetic Alphabet provides a single symbol for each sound in the language. In English, for example, where the pronunciation of a word so often fails to accord with the spelling, we thus have a method of making the pronunciation clear. Particularly in cases where a student cannot pronounce a word or is confused by the obscuring of certain syllables, it is helpful to be able to transcribe the word into phonetic script. Also, in teaching certain vowel sounds—particularly those which are peculiar to English—it is useful to have at hand a symbol to represent these sounds. By means of phonetic symbols, one can also indicate the voicing or unvoicing of terminal consonants, the existence of strong and weak forms, etc. These are all definite advantages.

Despite these advantages, as one goes down through the ranks of practicing teachers, one finds considerable disenchantment with the entire phonetic system of transcription now in use. Many teachers have conscientiously tried to use the IPA system in their work, only to find that the results did not justify the time spent, first, in teaching the various symbols themselves and, second, in adapting these symbols to the many subtleties of everyday English speech. Moreover, attempts to simplify the IPA system have not been particularly successful. One group of authorities has sponsored one set of changes; another group has recommended something quite different. While the general tendency toward simplification is to be commended, such unrelated changes only add to the confusion already felt by many teachers regarding the use of phonetic symbols in general.

Finally, the phonetic symbols in current school use, *without special qualifying markings,* fail to indicate in any way important differences between the production of many English sounds and the production of the corresponding sounds in other languages. English [t], for example, is not pronounced like Spanish [t]. English [p] is not pronounced like Spanish [p]. The sounds [t, d, p, b, k, g] are all aspirated in English and produced with a slightly different tongue position from that used in Spanish. English [l] and English [r] have little similarity to Spanish [l] and Spanish [r]. Yet the current phonetic symbols for [t, d, p, b, k, g, r, l] indicate no differences between the two corresponding sets of sounds. Consequently, English-speaking people will give to these symbols their own English pronunciation; Spanish-speaking people will give them a Spanish pronunciation—and both will assume that they are pronouncing the sounds correctly in the foreign language.

Classification of Speech Sounds

There are twenty-six letters in the English alphabet but upwards of some fifty different and distinct sounds. It is not our purpose or province here to describe all of these sounds or even to attempt to classify each of them. What follows below is merely a very general outline of the most important classes of English sounds. Some of the terms defined here appear frequently in later discussions. Therefore, we will describe such terms briefly at this point in order that the reader may understand more easily the material which follows. Any teacher who is interested in learning more about this general subject matter is referred to the various standard textbooks dealing with English speech.

The sounds of any language are generally divided into two main groups—vowels and consonants. All vowels are produced with voice, that is, with vibration of the vocal cords. They differ from consonants in that the outward flow of sound is largely unrestricted. In consonants, this flow is interrupted or diverted by one of the articulators—teeth, tongue, lips, soft palate.

There are anywhere from eleven to sixteen vowels in English, depending upon their classification. That is, the number depends not upon their possible production within the speech apparatus but upon their classification by different phoneticians. Some writers on phonetics recognize three vowels in the *a* group and four in the mid-vowel group. More recent writers tend toward some simplification of these and other groups. Phoneticians further classify vowels as *front*, *middle*, and *back* vowels, depending upon the position of the tongue in the mouth during production. Thus, [i], [ɪ], and [e] are front vowels, the tongue being in high front position when they are produced; [u], [ʊ], and [o] are back vowels; [ə] and [ɚ] are middle vowels.

Consonants are classified according to the manner of articulation as follows: (1) Stops or plosives. In the production of these sounds, the breath is checked in its outward movement, then suddenly released with a slight explosion. In this group fall the sounds [p, b, t, d, k, g]. (2) Continuants. A continuant is a sound which may be "continued" or prolonged as long as the speaker has breath to sustain it. Continuants are further divided into nasals [m, n, ŋ], laterals [l], and fricatives [f, v, h, w, θ, ð, s, z, ʃ, ʒ].

A further classification of consonants concerns their production in a voiced or voiceless manner. This is an important classification for our purposes, since the voicing or unvoicing of consonants, under certain specified conditions, is important in foreign accent correction. *Voiced consonants* are produced with vibration of the vocal cords. In this group we have [b, d, g, l, ð, v, z, ʒ]. *Unvoiced consonants* are produced with breath alone. These include [p, t, k, θ, f, s, ʃ].

It should be further observed that most voiced and unvoiced consonants fall into pairs, one consonant of the pair being voiced, and the other unvoiced. Thus *b* is voiced; *p* is unvoiced—although both sounds are otherwise produced alike. Such pairs may be grouped as follows:

| *Voiced* | b | d | g | v | z | ð | ʒ |
| *Unvoiced* | p | t | k | f | s | θ | ʃ |

Stress and Rhythm—Strong and Weak Forms

Stress is the emphasis given to a particular syllable within a word or to a particular word within a group of words. In individual words, stress is generally referred to as *accent*.

In English, as is generally known, words are very strongly accented. The accented syllable receives greater force than in most languages. The unaccented syllables, in turn, receive correspondingly less force. This tendency in English results in various phonetic changes. In emphasizing the accented syllable so strongly, we automatically sacrifice the vowel values in the remaining unstressed syllables. *It may be stated as a principle in English that all vowels, when occurring in unstressed syllables, are reduced from their normal values to the level of the neutral vowel* [ə]. For example, in the words *attempt* [ətɛ́mpt] and *contain* [kəntén], we can see clearly how this principle operates. The vowel of the unaccented syllable in each case is reduced from its normal value to the neutral [ə]. The only vowels which seem to resist this leveling tendency on occasion are the high front vowel [i] and the high back vowel [u]. Both these vowels are also reduced in unstressed syllables, but [i] is sometimes weakened only to [ɪ], as in *become* [bɪkə́m]; [u] is weakened to [ʊ], as in *July* [dʒʊldɑ́ɪ].

This important principle of English speech is often difficult for foreign students to understand. In their native language, students are often taught to respect the quality of all vowels. So, in speaking English, they naturally assume that if they pronounce each syllable clearly and exactly, they will be better understood. Actually, the reverse is true. Words in English are distinguishable by rhythm as well as by sound. Consequently, students will be much better understood if they stress the accented syllable strongly and totally obscure all remaining vowels.

Although consonants do not have strong and weak forms, they also undergo changes in value, just as vowels do. They are subject to the influence of stress. They are also influenced particularly by neighboring sounds, undergoing a process known as *assimilation*. Thus one sound may be altered by the sound which follows it (progressive assimilation). Another sound may be altered by the sound which precedes it (regressive assimilation). In the word *looked*, for example, the final voiced [d] follows a voiceless [k]. After pronouncing [k], it is so much easier for us to leave the vocal cords in relaxed position rather than to draw them together sharply for the normal voicing of the [d] that we end up by unvoicing the [d]. The word, though still retaining its spelling, is thus pronounced [lʊkt].

Actually, assimilation is a very common process, occurring in all languages. It results from a simple *law of economy*, whereby the organs of speech, instead of taking a new position for each sound, tend to draw sounds together with the purpose of saving time and energy. Assimilation becomes important in teaching English to foreign students only when the teacher fails to understand its operation and importance. Many teachers tend to follow the spelling of words and to teach overly precise forms rather than accepted assimilations. Thus some teachers will teach *picture* as [píktyʊr] rather than [píktʃɚ]. By analogy they then teach *nature* as [nétyur] instead of [nétʃɚ], *literature* as [lítɚətyʊr;] instead of [lítɚətʃɚ]. They teach *educate* as [ɛ́dyʊket] rather than [ɛ́dʒəket]. These same teachers are likely to claim that *did you*, pronounced [dídʒʊ], or *don't you*, pronounced [dóntʃʊ] are vulgarisms to be avoided in careful speech. Yet these forms occur in their own speech and in the speech of everyone who speaks everyday, normal English. Students, therefore, should be acquainted with these and comparable assimilations. Even if they can't use them in their own speech, they should at least be able to recognize and understand them in the speech of others.

We read above that all words of more than one syllable are strongly accented in English. That is, one syllable receives considerable stress, while the remaining syllables are weakened accordingly. *This same principle of accent holds true in phrases as well as in individual words.* In all phrases in English, one word or syllable is strongly accented. The remaining words or syllables receive correspondingly less stress. The vowels in all unstressed syllables are reduced from their original values to the neutral vowel [ə]. Unstressed one-syllable words such as articles, conjunctions, and pronouns are reduced to their corresponding *weak forms*. The article *an* [æn], for example, is weakened to [ən]. The conjunction *and* [ænd] becomes [ənd], *can* [kæn] becomes [kən] or even [kn]—etc.

It is easy for students (and teachers) to understand the accenting of individual words—but rarely do they understand the comparable accenting of phrases or thought groups. Yet when we speak, we always speak in phrases, not words. It is quite natural that we should accent the main or content words in a sentence and subordinate the less important elements.

It so happens that almost any phrase in English can be compared in its accent to some individual word. Thus, the phrase *in the morning* [inðəmórnɪŋ] is accented exactly as the word *eco-*

nomic [ikənámɪk]. The phrase *he's leaving* [hizlívɪŋ] carries the same accent as the word *appearing* [əpírɪŋ]. *I'll be there* [aɪlbɪðér] compares exactly in accent to *disappear* [dɪsəpír]. *He's been working* [hizbɪnwə́kɪŋ] is accented in the same way as the word *introduction* [ɪntrədə́kʃən]. A long list of such equally accented phrases and individual words can be drawn up by the teacher and used by the students for practice purposes.

Obviously, in special circumstances, one can alter the pattern of any phrase and emphasize a different word or syllable from the one normally stressed. If someone asks us, "Is the book *on* the table or *under* the table?" we might well reply "ON the table," stressing *on* rather than the first syllable of *table*, which is usually stressed. But this is a special situation which does not concern us here. *Remember this:* In normal, everyday, colloquial speech, all phrases carry a definite accent. Moreover, this accent, which grows out of the grammar of the language, is recurrent and stable. Thus any two native speakers of English, under normal circumstances, will read the same phrase in exactly the same way. In brief, to the American ear, the accent of any phrase is as clear and recognizable as the accent of any individual word. Finally—*and this is a very important point*—if any phrase is accented incorrectly, the error is just as great and just as obvious as when a word is accented on the wrong syllable.

Many times a foreign student, trying to be precise, will say, for example, "I *am* busy," putting stress on *am* instead of on the first syllable of *busy*, where it normally goes. The resulting distortion is just as noticeable (and just as confusing) as if the student, in pronouncing the word *Indiana* [ɪndiǽnə], mistakenly shifted the accent to the second syllable and said instead InDIana [ɪndíænə].

What we are discussing here is really rhythm. The succession of properly accented phrases in a sentence establishes what is known as the rhythm of a language. Rhythm is a definite and tangible phase of language. Rhythm provides a kind of musical framework for language. More important still, it also helps to convey meaning. In many cases, rhythm is as important in this respect as individual words or grammar.

Teachers may well ask how they should go about teaching stress and rhythm—if they have this importance. Clearly, they should not neglect more fundamental things to concentrate on stress and rhythm. Rhythm is a rather subtle matter. It is not easily grasped or appreciated by students, particularly on the elementary or lower intermediate levels. Yet there are a few obvious things which teachers, if they are interested, can do. First, they can show the relation between the accenting of many common phrases and individual words—as explained above. In this connection, they should be sure to emphasize the fact that we speak in phrases, not words, and that all phrases carry a definite accent, just as words do. The special exercises in this book on the proper stressing of phrases should prove helpful to teachers in this respect. Secondly, teachers can teach phrasing as part of the teaching of pronunciation. In reading practice sentences to the class, they can emphasize the stressing of accented syllables and the obscuring of vowels in all unaccented syllables. Students, in repeating such sentences after them, should follow the same rhythm patterns which they have emphasized. Again, the intonation exercises which appear in each lesson of this book should help to give the students the "feel" of most of the patterns into which English rhythm naturally falls. Thirdly, teachers can make use of the device of rhyming—particularly in teaching contracted verb forms such as *I'm, you're, we're, I'll, she'll, we've*, etc. Students fail to contract many of these forms sufficiently. They pronounce them as though they were composed of two syllables rather than a single syllable. Teachers can counteract this tendency by showing that *I'll* rhymes with *pile, he's* rhymes with *sneeze, I'm* rhymes with *time, we've* rhymes with *leave* —and so on. Fourthly, teachers can show students how English rhythm falls into certain definite patterns. These patterns grow out of the grammar of English, in accordance with the following general principles: *In speaking, we naturally stress so-called content words.* In most sentences, such words carry the burden of meaning. They include nouns, main verbs, descriptive adjectives, adverbs, demonstratives (*this, that, these, those*) and interrogatives (*who, which, why, when*, etc.).

In turn, we subordinate all function words, words which serve simply to define or show mood, direction, etc. The following are considered function words in English and, accordingly, are normally unstressed: definite and indefinite articles (*a, an, the*), personal pronouns (*I, you, he, my, your, his*, etc.), auxiliary verbs (*am, are, is, will, have, may, can*, etc.), relative pronouns (*who, which, that, whom*), and conjunctions (*and, but, although, if*, etc.).

Intonation

Intonation is the term used to describe the pitch or melody pattern of any group of words. The group of words involved is sometimes known as the intonation group. Pitch, in case the term is not familiar to the reader, is the position of a note on the musical scale. Pitch is determined by the frequency of vibration at which air waves strike the ear drum.

When there is an increase of stress on any one syllable, there is an accompanying rise in pitch on the same syllable. However, one should be careful to distinguish clearly between stress and pitch. Stress is associated with rhythm. Variations in stress give rise to rhythm in language. Stress patterns and the resultant rhythm, as we have seen, grow out of the grammar of a language. Thus rhythm is stable and fairly predictable.

Changes in pitch, on the other hand, result in varying intonation patterns. Pitch is often a personal or individual matter—especially on advanced levels. Pitch and the resultant intonation thus show a great variation in form. In addition, they frequently carry various emotional overtones.

The following two principles govern all basic intonation patterns in English. Actually, these two principles are really all foreign students need to know about intonation and all they need to be taught:

1. The first principle requires that all completed statements, including commands, end with a downward glide of the voice on the last accented syllable. This type of intonation is known as rising-falling intonation. It is used for all statements and commands. The fall of the voice at the end of a sentence indicates to the listener that the speaker has terminated and no answer or further comment is necessarily expected.

2. The second principle is that all statements indicating incompleteness, doubt, or hesitation end with an upward glide of the voice on the last accented syllable. In this category are included all questions which may be answered yes or no. This type of into-

nation is known as rising intonation. Questions beginning with interrogative words such as *when, where, why,* since these words in themselves indicate that the statement is a question, generally follow the first principle.

In this book, the following system of intonation is used: There are three tones involved—normal, high, and low. A line drawn directly at the base of a word shows that the word is pronounced with a normal tone; a line just above the word indicates a high tone; a line well below the level of a word indicates a low tone.

a) The following are examples of type one intonation—that is, rising-falling intonation. Note that the high note generally coincides with the last stressed syllable of the sentence.

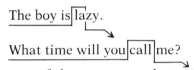

Note that in some of the sentences where rising-falling intonation occurs, the last sentence stress may fall on a word of only one syllable. In such cases, there is no room for the low note to follow. An inflection of the voice then occurs, indicated by an angled line.

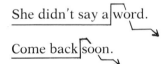

b) The following is an example of type two intonation—namely, rising intonation.

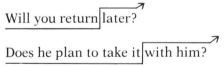

Aspiration

Aspiration is the term given to the slight puff of air, like a [h], which follows the production of [p], [t], and [k] in English. This aspiration is strongest when [p], [t], and [k] are in initial position in a stressed syllable and followed by a vowel, as in the words *pen* [pɛn] and *suspend* [səspɛ́nd]. It is weak when the sounds are in final position after a consonant which is often unreleased, as in *sent* [sɛnt]. It is weakest when the sounds occur in medial position;

here the puff of air is so slight as to be hardly perceptible—as in *happy* [hǽpɪ].

This aspiration is not a fundamental part of these sounds—which are all voiceless plosives. As may be seen from what has just been said, the aspiration varies in intensity with the position of the sound. When [p], [t], and [k] are followed by a consonant in the same breath group, the puff does not occur at all—for example, *pride* [prɑɪd]. Yet the aspiration remains a very important characteristic of each of these sounds, especially if the sound is in initial position. For one thing, the aspiration serves to distinguish the sounds from their voiced cognates [b], [d], and [g]. The sound [p], for example, is more than merely the unvoiced counterpart (cognate) of [b]. It is unvoiced [b], with a distinctive aspiration added. This aspiration is clearly noticeable to the American ear and helps substantially in identifying the sound.

The same aspiration of these sounds does not occur in German, in the Slavic languages, or in any of the Romance languages. Consequently, most foreign students studying English pay little attention to it. Generally the students do not hear the aspiration clearly. Even in cases where they hear it, they are unable to reproduce it. Yet no error is more noticeable in the speech of foreign students. It is an error which clings to the speech of even the most advanced students.

To the person not trained in speech, the difference between an aspirated [t] and an unaspirated [t] may not seem a very significant one. Yet the failure to aspirate comes through very clearly in English speech, causing a heavy, blunt effect which is definitely non-English. Compare the pronunciation of *ten* (the numeral) in English and *ten* (the imperative form of *tener*) in Spanish. There sometimes results a definite confusion of words if the necessary aspiration is lacking. In rapid speech, unaspirated [p] sounds like voiced [b]; unaspirated [t] sounds like [d]; unaspirated [k] like [g]. Foreign students say *ten* without aspirating the [t], and native listeners think they are saying *den*. Foreign students say *pie*, and it sounds to native listeners like *by*.

This error, in general, is fairly easy to correct once teachers understand the principle involved and the facts are made clear to the students. Teachers should first show the students how strong the aspiration of [p], [t], and [k] is in their own speech. They should pass among the students repeating such words as *pen, ten, come.* They can exaggerate the aspiration on [p], [t], and [k] slightly—though this is not really necessary since the aspiration on these sounds, even in normal speech, is considerable. They can let students feel with the backs of their hands the strong puff of air which is emitted each time they (the teachers) pronounce [p], [t], and [k]. Students are generally amazed at the really strong aspiration given to these sounds. Or teachers can hold a small piece of paper lightly in front of their mouths as they speak. The paper will flutter each time they say [p], [t], or [k]. A match flame, held before the mouth, shows the same effect.

After this, it is just a matter of practice on the students' part to learn this important principle of aspiration. Students should repeat aloud simple words beginning with [p]—*pen, pay, pour, put, pear.* Later they should practice with simple words beginning with [t] and [k]. At first, students can hold pieces of paper before their mouths to show the amount of aspiration taking place. However, this soon becomes unnecessary because the sharp difference between the aspirated and unaspirated forms of these sounds is presently clear to all. From this point on, it is just a matter of correction each time a student fails to aspirate [p], [t], or [k] sufficiently.

Voicing and Unvoicing of Final Consonants

Another serious error of the foreign student learning English is the failure, in required circumstances, to voice final consonants. We have already learned the difference between voiced and unvoiced consonants. (See page 11.) The particular voiced consonants which concern us here are [b, d, g, v, z, ð, ʒ]. Their unvoiced counterparts are [p, t, k, f, s, θ, ʃ].

In rapid speech, it is sometimes difficult to tell whether a consonant is voiced or unvoiced. This simple test may be used. Stop the ears while sounding alternately any such pairs as *fife* and *five*, prolonging the final sounds of *f* and *v*. In holding the sound *f* by itself, one will hear only a fricative rustling of the breath as it passes the teeth and lips. In sounding *v*, this same friction is heard with the addition of voice, the vibration of the vocal cords.

In English, all voiced consonants occurring at the end of a word are generally held and voiced. In German and the Slavic and Romance languages, the opposite situation prevails. All voiced consonants, when occurring in terminal position, are automatically unvoiced. For example, in Russian the name *Chekhov*, although terminating in *v*, a voiced consonant, is pronounced [tʃékɔf]. In accordance with the rules of Russian, the final [v] is automatically unvoiced and changed into its unvoiced counterpart [f]. In English this same word would normally be pronounced [tʃékɔv]. The final [v] would be held and voiced. Compare the English pronunciation of *love* [ləv], *move* [muv], and *of* [əv].

Foreign students, in bringing to English the habits of speech acquired in their native languages, naturally tend to unvoice all final voiced consonants. The effect in English, however, is unfortunate. Students, instead of saying *his* [hɪz], say [hɪs]. Instead of saying *have* [hæv], they say [hæf]. For *bag* [bæg], they say [bæk]—and so on. The list of such possible distortions, where foreign students turn final [d] into [t], final [g] into [k], final [v] into [f], and so forth, is almost endless. In some cases, actual confusion of words results. If students, in pronouncing *bad*, unvoice the final [d] and change it to [t], they come out with *bat*. In such a case, they have changed not only the form of the word but also its meaning. There are many pairs of English words distinguishable only by the voicing or unvoicing of the final consonant. Consider —to name just a few—*bed, bet; need, neat; feed, feet; buzz, bus; grows, gross; rise, rice; raise, race; pays, pace; leave, leaf; bag, back*.

As may be readily seen, it is very important to hold and voice all such final voiced consonants in English. This voicing sometimes varies in intensity, but this fact need not concern foreign students. The principles involved should first be explained to the students so that they understand what they are doing. Then they should be drilled carefully on matching pairs of words such as those which appear above. They should also be given practice with phrases and short sentences containing final voiced consonants. It is sometimes helpful if it is explained to students that all vowels preceding final voiced consonants are somewhat lengthened in duration. That is, all vowels are held slightly longer before final voiced consonants than before final unvoiced consonants. The [æ] in *bad*, for example, is of longer duration than the [æ] in *bat*. The [ɛ] in *bed* is held longer than the [ɛ] of *bet*, etc.

INTERNATIONAL PHONETIC ALPHABET*

Consonants

[p]—pie, hope, happy
[b]—bell, bite, globe
[f]—fine, office
[v]—vest, of, have
[k]—keep, can, book
[g]—go, get, egg
[l]—let, little, lay
[m]—man, must, dime
[n]—no, down, ton
[ŋ]—sing, ringing
[w]—water, we, one
[θ]—thin, three, path

[ð]—they, then, other
[s]—see, sat, city
[z]—zoo, does, is
[ʃ]—shoe, ship, action
[ʒ]—usual, garage
[tʃ]—chance, watch
[dʒ]—June, edge
[r]—red, rich, write
[y]—you, yes, million
[h]—he, hat, who
[t]—ten, to, meet
[d]—do, did

Vowels and Diphthongs

[ɪ]—it, did, build
[i]—me, see, people
[ɛ]—end, let, any
[æ]—cat, bat, laugh
[ɑ]—army, father, hot
[ɔ]—all, caught, long
[ʊ]—book, full, took
[u]—too, move, fruit

[ə]—cup, soda, infant
[ɚ]—her, work, bird
[e]—say, they, mail
[o]—old, coal, sew
[aɪ]—dry, eye, buy
[ɔɪ]—toy, boy, soil
[aʊ]—cow, our, house

In accordance with common practice and for reasons of simplification, these minor changes in symbols have been introduced. [ə] and [ɚ] are used in this book for both stressed and unstressed syllables. [y] is used instead of IPA [j]. [ɑ] is used instead of IPA [a].

NOTES ON THE MARKINGS

1. An arrow pointing up or down at the end of a sentence indicates a slight rise or fall in intonation.

   Did you hear that?

   They've been friends for years.

2. A stress mark over a word or syllable indicates that it should be spoken with more strength or force, obscuring some of the surrounding syllables.

   It was a bad móvie.

3. The example sound is underlined both in the table of contents and in the box at the beginning of each lesson.

   t as in ten, center, might

4. In the Table of Contents, in the boxes at the beginning of each lesson, in the second and third lists of homonyms, and in the list of words with silent letters, silent letters are marked with a dot underneath them.

   t as in ten, center, might

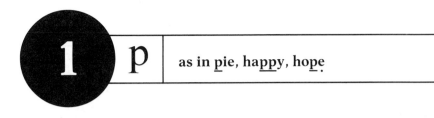

1 p   as in p͟ie, ha͟pp͟y, hop͟e

I. PRONUNCIATION

To make this sound, close your lips, then voicelessly blow them open with a puff of air according to the guidelines in the Preface.

pear	people	top
pick	September	hip
pet	apple	pep
palm	purple	nap
part	complete	cap
poor	apartment	soup

II. COMPARISON

Practice these contrasting sounds.

bear	pear		big	pig
rib	rip		bath	path
cab	cap		bay	pay
be	pea		bet	pet

III. REPETITION

1. The paper was printed and published without profit.
2. We had to learn both the past and present tense of all the verbs.
3. Paula carefully put the apples and peaches in the basket.
4. Our plan was opposed by almost everyone present.
5. Drops of water kept dripping from the roof.
6. The umpire, now in a bad mood, argued loudly with the player.

7. Both the interest and the principal must be paid in September.
8. His only hope of escape lay through the opening in the fence.

IV. PHRASING AND INTONATION

a. Blend together the words in each of these phrases to form a single unit—that is, pronounce each phrase as though it were a single word. Also stress the accented syllable strongly, obscuring the vowels in the remaining syllables.

a bad púppy	much better próse	to play báll
a big táble	a pretty bírd	my best cáp
to say nóthing	to take a náp	in the párk

b. The teacher reads each of the following sentences in a normal manner, giving some slight emphasis to phrasing and intonation. Students repeat after teacher. Teacher repeats after students.

1. (Teacher)   They played in the park all afternoon.

   (Students)   They played in the park all afternoon.
   (Teacher)   They played in the park all afternoon.

2. (Teacher)   Why didn't you buy some apples?

   (Students)   Why didn't you buy some apples?
   (Teacher)   Why didn't you buy some apples?

3. (Teacher)   Do you prefer pork or beef?

   (Students)   Do you prefer pork or beef?
   (Teacher)   Do you prefer pork or beef?

Teacher and students continue in exactly the same manner with these sentences: Teacher reads, students repeat, teacher repeats.

4. Paul practiced playing the piano all morning.
5. I prefer peaches, but Peter likes plums.
6. I don't play bridge, but I like to watch others play.
7. What department does Peter work in?
8. Peter now works in the printing department.
9. Where did you buy that pretty playsuit?
10. I bought it in Pratt's Department Store.

V. REVIEW DIALOGUE

- Hello, Tip. This is your old pal, Paul Sipe. I'm calling you from a place near Pittsburgh, Pennsylvania.
- Hi, Paul. Are you still playing the piano?
- I'm unhappy to say that I've stopped playing.
- I hope the pains in your fingers aren't keeping you from playing.
- No, I'm just too busy with my new job as a police officer in the first precinct. It's on Peach Street. Get some paper so you can write down my new address.
- Certainly. When you get settled, Pat and I want you to come over to supper. I've got a great new recipe for pecan pie.

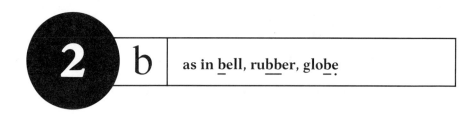

2 **b** | as in <u>b</u>ell, ru<u>bb</u>er, glo<u>b</u>e

I. PRONUNCIATION

To make this sound, close your lips as you did with the [p] sound, but press them firmly; then open them and produce a voiced sound, but no puff of air.

be	about	job
big	rabbit	rib
bet	subscription	cab
bat	subtract	rob
barn	subject	robe
boot	able	rub

II. COMPARISON

Practice these contrasting sounds.

rib	rip		by	pie
cab	cap		bill	pill
bark	park		bath	path
back	pack		ball	Paul

III. REPETITION

1. The brass band played so loudly that we could barely hear each other.
2. The boys assembled in groups about a block apart.
3. The cab stopped at the curb, and the cab driver jumped out.

4. It was too big a job for Benny to do.
5. The waitress brought us bread but no butter.
6. It was by far the best ball game of the season.
7. The boys hid behind the back fence.
8. The rabbit ran into a hole behind the barn.

IV. PHRASING AND INTONATION

a. Blend together the words in each of these phrases to form a single unit—that is, pronounce each phrase as though it were a single word. Also stress the accented syllable strongly, obscuring the vowels in the remaining syllables.

a bright pín	to buy a péncil	to bake a píe
a big bíll	to pay a dóllar	a paper bág
to play brídge		a broken pláte

b. The teacher reads each of the following sentences in a normal manner, giving some slight emphasis to phrasing and intonation. Students repeat after teacher. Teacher repeats after students.

1. (Teacher) Barbara was a very pretty bride.

   (Students) Barbara was a very pretty bride.
   (Teacher) Barbara was a very pretty bride.

2. (Teacher) What subject were they talking about?

   (Students) What subject were they talking about?
   (Teacher) What subject were they talking about?

3. (Teacher) Were you able to reach Mr. Brown?

   (Students) Were you able to reach Mr. Brown?
   (Teacher) Were you able to reach Mr. Brown?

Teacher and students continue in exactly the same manner with these sentences: Teacher reads, students repeat, teacher repeats.

4. Where did you buy those rubber boots?
5. I bought them in Brown's Department Store.
6. When is the boy's next birthday?
7. He was born in the month of February.
8. Have all the big bills for this month been paid?
9. Ben has a good job at the bank.
10. At the banquet I sat between Betty and Bob.

V. REVIEW DIALOGUE

- What are you boys doing in the building this early in the morning?
- We're practicing, Ms. Cobb. Some of us are on the basketball team, and some of us are in the band.
- Which band is that, Bobby?
- We call ourselves The Suburbs. Both the boys and the girls here at Benjamin Banneker High School like the beat of our music. I play this big, brass tuba. Do you want to hear me?
- I'll bet you're wonderful, Bobby, but I'd better get to the biology lab before the bell rings.
- We'll be in class on time. Biology is my favorite subject, but before we go to class, we have to practice our theme song, "The Suburbs are Back."

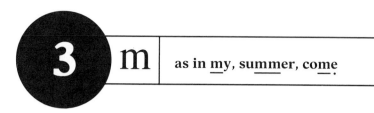

3 | m | as in <u>m</u>y, sum<u>m</u>er, co<u>m</u>e

I. PRONUNCIATION

To make this sound, press your lips tightly together and voice a hum.

man	company	some
men	empty	home
make	summer	time
may	games	come
me	famous	arm
my	almost	from

II. COMPARISON

Practice these contrasting sounds.

mice	nice	some	sun
gum	gun	warm	warn
meet	neat	dime	dine
mime	mine	them	then

III. REPETITION

1. They may remain here until March.
2. Martin's work may mean a good promotion for him in time.
3. He comes from a family of moderate income.
4. The smell of smoke was so strong that many people began to move toward the exits.

5. His fame was limited to a few minor headlines in the daily papers.
6. He lives in a one-room apartment in the middle of town.
7. They walked home arm in arm.
8. The warm summer sun made everyone very uncomfortable.

IV. PHRASING AND INTONATION

a. Blend together the words in each of these phrases or sentences to form a single unit—that is, pronounce each phrase as though it were a single word. Also stress the accented syllable strongly, obscuring the vowels in the remaining syllables.

among the bóoks	bóth of them	to make móney
I may be láte.	áll of it	will come láter
from time to tíme	dóne with it	feels much bétter

b. The teacher reads each of the following sentences in a normal manner, giving some slight emphasis to phrasing and intonation. Students repeat after teacher. Teacher repeats after students.

1. (Teacher)   Have you met my mother and brother?

    (Students)   Have you met my mother and brother?
    (Teacher)   Have you met my mother and brother?

2. (Teacher)   No, but I'm very glad to meet them.

    (Students)   No, but I'm very glad to meet them.
    (Teacher)   No, but I'm very glad to meet them.

3. (Teacher)   Why don't you come to our home for dinner?

    (Students)   Why don't you come to our home for dinner?
    (Teacher)   Why don't you come to our home for dinner?

Teacher and students continue in exactly the same manner with these sentences: Teacher reads, students repeat, teacher repeats.

4. I'd like to come very much.
5. May I offer you some lemonade?
6. What was the name of that author we were speaking about?
7. Do you mean Somerset Maugham, by any chance?
8. Must the children make so much noise?
9. What country do Mr. and Mrs. Martinez come from?
10. They are Mexicans but have lived for many years in Montana.

V. REVIEW DIALOGUE

- Good morning. My name is Michael Morris, and this is my son Max.
- I think I remember you from last year, Mr. Morris. You're the mattress merchant from Manhattan, aren't you?
- We used to live in Manhattan, but last month we moved our home to Vermont. Sometimes we come down here to visit old friends and to shop.
- What may I do for you and Max today?
- At the end of this summer—no later than September—we'll be moving again. This time we're moving to Maine. We want to buy some paintings for the living room, and we want you to mail them to our new home.
- If there's anything we can do to make your move more comfortable, just let me know.

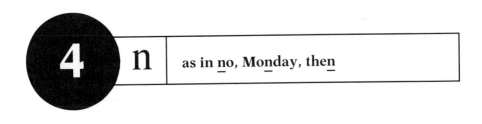

4 **n** as in <u>n</u>o, Mo<u>n</u>day, the<u>n</u>

I. PRONUNCIATION

To make this sound, open your mouth and raise the tip of your tongue to the upper gum ridge. Keep the sides of your tongue touching the inside of the upper teeth, and send a voiced sound through your nose.

no	any	green
name	only	been
new	morning	ran
never	raining	than
noon	window	train
not	into	down

II. COMPARISON

Practice these contrasting sounds.

neck	deck	dine	died
nor	door	pan	pad
near	dear	pain	paid
net	debt	train	trade

III. REPETITION

1. They need have no fear of our refusing to help them.
2. A number of new applications have been sent.
3. I had telephoned him at least nine or ten times.

4. The news that the governor had spent the night in New York was not reported in the newspapers.
5. Though opportunity may knock only once for some people, it seems to knock quite often for others.
6. We received no news from them for nearly a month.
7. The work will be finished by next November.
8. We never know when to expect him.

IV. PHRASING AND INTONATION

a. Blend together the words in each of these phrases or sentences to form a single unit—that is, pronounce each phrase as though it were a single word. Also stress the accented syllable strongly, obscuring the vowels in the remaining syllables.

a rainy dáy	very noisy néighbors	Go ask Dád.
nothing at áll	dirty, dusty córners	late at níght
night after níght	lost but happy chíldren	there's none léft

b. The teacher reads each of the following sentences in a normal manner, giving some slight emphasis to phrasing and intonation. Students repeat after teacher. Teacher repeats after students.

1. (Teacher)   Have you ever known such a noisy person?

   (Students)   Have you ever known such a noisy person?
   (Teacher)   Have you ever known such a noisy person?

2. (Teacher)   What color is your new dress—green?

   (Students)   What color is your new dress—green?
   (Teacher)   What color is your new dress—green?

3. (Teacher)   It's raining too hard to go out.

   (Students)   It's raining too hard to go out.
   (Teacher)   It's raining too hard to go out.

Teacher and students continue in exactly the same manner with these sentences: Teacher reads, students repeat, teacher repeats.

4. Ned was nineteen on his last birthday.
5. When did Nathan join the navy?
6. The Nelsons are leaving for Nevada tomorrow.
7. Nora never gets up before noon.
8. Ned takes a nap nearly every afternoon.
9. Did Dan earn any money during the summer?
10. We knocked and knocked, but no one answered.

V. SPECIAL INTONATION PATTERNS

Although the high note in any normally spoken sentence falls on the final stressed syllable, sometimes it is necessary to raise the pitch on some other syllable in order to give emphasis to a particular idea. For example, let us consider the sentence: *When are they leaving for Chicago?* Without any particular intonation stress, the sentence might well appear rather indefinite as to meaning. However, we can convey whatever idea the speaker has in mind simply by raising the pitch on the indicated syllable.

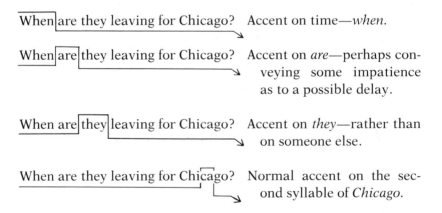

When are they leaving for Chicago? Accent on time—*when.*

When are they leaving for Chicago? Accent on *are*—perhaps conveying some impatience as to a possible delay.

When are they leaving for Chicago? Accent on *they*—rather than on someone else.

When are they leaving for Chicago? Normal accent on the second syllable of *Chicago.*

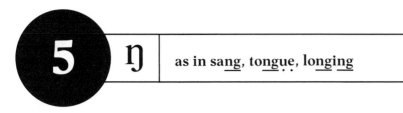

5 **ŋ** as in sa<u>ng</u>, to<u>ngu</u>e, lo<u>ng</u>i<u>ng</u>

I. PRONUNCIATION

To make this sound, raise the back of your tongue toward the soft palate and voice a nasal sound. Do not let your tongue touch the roof of your mouth.

sing	laughing	hungry
bring	coming	English
ring	going	language
long	making	stronger
thing	doing	younger
wing	waiting	angry

II. COMPARISON

Practice these contrasting sounds.

ting	tin	
thing	thin	
wing	win	
sing	sin	
hang	hand	ham

III. REPETITION

1. We were hoping to get one of the remaining single seats.
2. The men were getting tired of eating such poor food.
3. I had a feeling that we were taking the wrong road.

4. She will try anything to bring attention to herself.
5. A strong breeze was beginning to blow all along the shore.
6. Mr. Kingsley has been hoping to make a living by writing short stories.
7. It had been a long, long time since we had heard such good singing.
8. They have both been studying English since coming to the United States.

IV. PHRASING AND INTONATION

a. Blend together the words in each of these phrases or sentences to form a single unit—that is, pronounce each phrase as though it were a single word. Also stress the accented syllable strongly, obscuring the vowels in the remaining syllables.

Send a télegram.　　It's David Wílson.　　What a thing to sáy!
I'll be seéing you.　　The English lánguage　　What a pretty dáy!

b. The teacher reads each of the following sentences in a normal manner, giving some slight emphasis to phrasing and intonation. Students repeat after teacher. Teacher repeats after students.

1. (Teacher)　Are you going on a singing tour this spring?

   (Students)　Are you going on a singing tour this spring?
   (Teacher)　Are you going on a singing tour this spring?

2. (Teacher)　His younger brother is stronger than he is.

   (Students)　His younger brother is stronger than he is.
   (Teacher)　His younger brother is stronger than he is.

3. (Teacher)　Why is the baby crying so much?

   (Students)　Why is the baby crying so much?
   (Teacher)　Why is the baby crying so much?

Teacher and students continue in exactly the same manner with these sentences: Teacher reads, students repeat, teacher repeats.

4. A bee stung her on the finger.
5. Where is everybody going?
6. Everyone's going swimming. Don't you want to come along?
7. No, thanks. I'm not feeling well today.
8. Is the English language difficult to learn?
9. English grammar is easy, but English spelling and pronunciation are a little harder.
10. I have been trying to reach you all day long.

V. REVIEW DIALOGUE

- Spelling has been hard for me ever since I was a young girl. Please help me with the spelling of your name.
- Certainly, Miss King. It's Irving Orange. I-r-v-i-n-g O-r-a-n-g-e, just like the color.
- Thank you. What are you doing?
- I'm drinking some ginger ale. Would you like some?
- No, thanks. I'm going to take a singing lesson, and I want my throat to be clear.
- You seem to have a strong voice. How long have you been taking singing lessons?
- Since I started studying English—about three years.

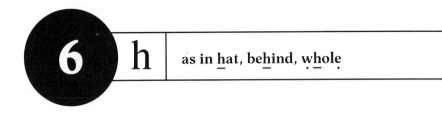

6 **h** as in <u>h</u>at, be<u>h</u>ind, <u>wh</u>ole

I. PRONUNCIATION

To make this sound, open your mouth and sigh voicelessly in a relaxed manner.

heat	him	behind
have	her	perhaps
hat	hide	anyhow
help	his	behave
hear	who	unhappy
hello	how	ahead

II. COMPARISON

Practice these contrasting sounds.

hat	at		hair	air
hear	ear		his	is
hand	and		heat	eat
hit	it		hall	all

III. REPETITION

1. The horse had difficulty hauling the heavy load.
2. The house had not been inhabited for many years.
3. Who told Heather that her horse was from Haiti?
4. Harry had a huge hole in the heel of his stocking.
5. Perhaps Hillary will take the job in Honduras anyhow.

6. They built their new home on a high hill above the town.
7. You can hang your hat on that hook in the hall.
8. Mr. Harris had given us no hint of his plan to hire Holly to help him in his office.

IV. PHRASING AND INTONATION

a. Blend together the words in each of these phrases or sentences to form a single unit—that is, pronounce each phrase as though it were a single word. Also stress the accented syllable strongly, obscuring the vowels in the remaining syllables.

in a húrry   Is it reády yet?   a table for twó
time for dínner   Have you órdered yet?   He's hurrying hóme.

b. The teacher reads each of the following sentences in a normal manner, giving some slight emphasis to phrasing and intonation. Students repeat after teacher. Teacher repeats after students.

1. (Teacher)   Why is Helen so happy today?

   (Students) Why is Helen so happy today?
   (Teacher)   Why is Helen so happy today?

2. (Teacher)   Hank has a new hat and new shoes.

   (Students) Hank has a new hat and new shoes.
   (Teacher)   Hank has a new hat and new shoes.

3. (Teacher)   Have you ordered your lunch yet?

   (Students) Have you ordered your lunch yet?
   (Teacher)   Have you ordered your lunch yet?

Teacher and students continue in exactly the same manner with these sentences: Teacher reads, students repeat, teacher repeats.

4. Not yet, but we both want ham and eggs.
5. Why are the children hurrying home?
6. They're hurrying home because it looks like rain.
7. Who is that man in the high hat?
8. That's Professor Harris, the head of the history department.

V. SHIFTS OF ACCENT

There are a few infallible rules of accent in English. Note, too, that in some instances the same word is accented differently, depending on its form. The noun *récord*, for example, shifts its accent to the second syllable when used as the verb *recórd*.

Noun Form	Verb Form	Noun Form	Verb Form	Other Examples
áddict	addíct	cómpress	compréss	pérfect (adjective)
álly	allý	súrvey	survéy	perféct (verb)
próduce	prodúce	récall	recáll	compáct (adjective)
cónvert	convért	súspect	suspéct	cómpact (noun)
óbject	objéct	cónflict	conflíct	compléx (adjective)
pérmit	permít			cómplex (noun)
présent	presént			fréquent (adjective)
cónduct	condúct			frequént (verb)

In the following corresponding noun and adjective forms of some common English words, notice how in some cases the accent remains the same in both the adjective and noun forms. In others, it shifts from one syllable in the adjective form to another syllable in the noun form.

Adjective Form	Noun Form	Adjective Form	Noun Form
ínnocent	ínnocence	póssible	possibílity
dífferent	dífference	sympathétic	sýmpathy
convénient	convénience	ánxious	anxíety
suspícious	suspícion	génerous	generósity
beáutiful	beáuty	símple	simplícity
		régular	regulárity
		mystérious	mýstery

7 hw as in <u>wh</u>y, <u>wh</u>isper, some<u>wh</u>ere

I. PRONUNCIATION

To make this sound, round your lips and blow out making a voiceless sound.

which	whiskers	nowhere
where	whiskey	somewhere
why	whisper	anywhere
when	whip	somewhat
what	whether	meanwhile
white	whistle	everywhere

II. COMPARISON

Practice these contrasting sounds.

which	witch		where	hair
whether	weather		when	hen
where	wear		wheat	heat
			white	height

III. REPETITION

1. The white snow fell softly to the ground.
2. Where and when did William get such an idea?
3. His well-cut white whiskers gave him a distinguished look.
4. Everywhere we went, we wondered if we'd be recognized; we were somewhat frightened.

5. Meanwhile, the books which we had been waiting for were delivered somewhere else.
6. We whistled and whistled, but we were not sure whether anyone heard us.
7. No one knew when or why he had left.
8. In the story of Moby Dick, Captain Ahab looks everywhere for the white whale.

IV. PHRASING AND INTONATION

a. Blend together the words in each of these phrases or sentences to form a single unit—that is, pronounce each phrase as though it were a single word. Also stress the accented syllable strongly, obscuring the vowels in the remaining syllables.

white wíne	Why wáit for her?	Tell Sálly to try it.
right nów	Don't pláy with it.	Why wórry about it?

b. The teacher reads each of the following sentences in a normal manner, giving some slight emphasis to phrasing and intonation. Students repeat after teacher. Teacher repeats after students.

1. (Teacher) Which do you prefer — white bread or wheat?

   (Students) Which do you prefer — white bread or wheat?

   (Teacher) Which do you prefer — white bread or wheat?

2. (Teacher) Have you decided where to go?

   (Students) Have you decided where to go?
   (Teacher) Have you decided where to go?

3. (Teacher) We painted all the woodwork white.

(Students)   We painted all the woodwork white.
(Teacher)   We painted all the woodwork white.

Teacher and students continue in exactly the same manner with these sentences: Teacher reads, students repeat, teacher repeats.

4.   I don't see our waiter anywhere.
5.   What is the name of the woman in the white wheelchair?
6.   What did you do when you were in Wheeling, West Virginia?
7.   While we were there, we learned to whistle.
8.   Whenever my sister and I whisper to each other, our mother tells us to stop.

V. HOMONYMS

A homonym is a word spelled differently but pronounced the same as another word. The [hw] sound in this lesson, such as in words like *where*, *which*, and *what*, produces a slight puff of air in the initial sound. If a piece of paper were held to the lips and these words were spoken, the paper would move slightly. No such puff of air would be noticeable in the words *wear*, *witch*, and *watt*.

Many native English speakers, however, make no distinction between the two sounds [hw] and [w]. The words *whether* and *weather* sound the same; that is, they are homonyms. There is usually no confusion in pronouncing homonyms since people can tell from the context of the sentence which word is intended.

where	wear		wheel	we'll
which	witch		whine	wine
whether	weather		whit	wit

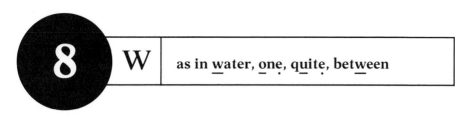

8 | **W** | as in <u>w</u>ater, <u>o</u>ne, qui<u>t</u>e, bet<u>w</u>een

I. PRONUNCIATION

To make this sound, keep your tongue high and back (at the beginning of the sound), round your lips and push them forward, and blow out with a voiced sound.

west	weather	away
way	won	twenty
work	wise	awake
wide	water	forward
warm	went	backward
wind	word	sandwich

II. COMPARISON

Practice these contrasting sounds.

wear	where		west	vest
witch	which		wine	vine
Y	why		worse	verse
			wow	vow

III. REPETITION

1. We decided to wait one week for Warren's answer.
2. A warm wind blew strongly from the west.
3. The change from warm to cold weather came without warning.

4. Wendy wanted to wear western clothes on Wednesday.
5. I love to walk through the woods in the winter.
6. We want to write the new words in our notebooks.
7. In some places the wall was wider than it was high.
8. We visit William once a week, but he's always away.

IV. PHRASING AND INTONATION

a. Blend together the words in each of these phrases to form a single unit—that is, pronounce each phrase as though it were a single word. Also stress the accented syllable strongly, obscuring the vowels in the remaining syllables.

very wet wéather	return the kéy	a blue póster
backward and fórward	to lie awáke	a wide válley

b. The teacher reads each of the following sentences in a normal manner, giving some slight emphasis to phrasing and intonation. Students repeat after teacher. Teacher repeats after students.

1. (Teacher) Isn't this weather rather warm for winter?

   (Students) Isn't this weather rather warm for winter?
   (Teacher) Isn't this weather rather warm for winter?

2. (Teacher) We had to wait three weeks for his answer.

   (Students) We had to wait three weeks for his answer.
   (Teacher) We had to wait three weeks for his answer.

3. (Teacher) How long did they stay there?

   (Students) How long did they stay there?
   (Teacher) How long did they stay there?

Teacher and students continue in exactly the same manner with these sentences: Teacher reads, students repeat, teacher repeats.

4. The weather is warm, but the wind is cold.
5. Do you like to walk in the woods alone?
6. I waited a week for them to fix my watch.
7. William has a new wrist watch which he bought in Woolworth's.
8. What are you watching through that window?
9. I'm watching those workmen argue with one another.
10. Although Wednesday was a cold, windy day, we all went to the wedding.

V. REVIEW DIALOGUE

- What's the weather like today, Wanda?
- Windy and cold, Walter. In fact, there are freezing winds and rain all along the western part of West Virginia.
- I wish the road we'll be taking weren't so winding; when it gets wet, it also gets very slippery.
- You're going to West Virginia with your wife for the weekend, aren't you? One day Warren and I must visit you there.
- That's a good idea, but we should wait until it's not quite so cold. Winnie and I take walks in the woods, but I think it would be too cold for you and Warren. Let's wait until the weather is warmer.
- Good idea. Now, let's see if you have everything—wrist watch, twin-blade razor, sandwiches, and a water canteen for the road —I guess you're ready.

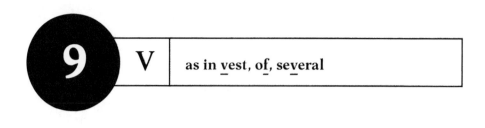

I. PRONUNCIATION

To make this sound, touch the inside of your lower lip with your upper front teeth and make a voiced sound.

vine	clever	love
very	river	leave
vote	cover	give
visit	favor	live
value	flavor	above
vest	never	remove

II. COMPARISON

Practice these contrasting sounds.

believe	belief		vowel	bowel
veal	we'll		very	berry
prove	proof		verve	verb
vat	fat		halve	half

III. REPETITION

1. We all voted in favor of the longer vacation.
2. The governor will veto the bill within five days.
3. We have a fine view of the valley from our front window.
4. We will leave for Virginia at five o'clock.
5. The heavy waves overturned the small vessel.
6. What places will you visit during your vacation?

7. The singer's voice proved to be well above average.
8. Vera wore a long veil which covered her whole face.

IV. PHRASING AND INTONATION

a. Blend together the words in each of these phrases to form a single unit—that is, pronounce each phrase as though it were a single word. Also stress the accented syllable strongly, obscuring the vowels in the remaining syllables.

to live wéll	a pleasant vóice	the Volga Ríver
to save tíme	to fall in lóve	a long vacátion

b. The teacher reads each of the following sentences in a normal manner, giving some slight emphasis to phrasing and intonation. Students repeat after teacher. Teacher repeats after students.

1. (Teacher) Why don't we ever go the movies?

   (Students) Why don't we ever go to the movies?
   (Teacher) Why don't we ever go to the movies?

2. (Teacher) We don't like the movies.

   (Students) We don't like the movies.
   (Teacher) We don't like the movies.

3. (Teacher) Will the president veto the bill?

   (Students) Will the president veto the bill?
   (Teacher) Will the president veto the bill?

Teacher and students continue in exactly the same manner with these sentences: Teacher reads, students repeat, teacher repeats.

4. Have you ever written any verse?
5. Why did Vera leave school early?

6. Some friends are visiting them over the weekend.
7. They live in a small village in Virginia.
8. To whom should we give the money?
9. Give it either to Victor or to Vera.
10. They plan to spend their vacation in Vermont.

V. REVIEW DIALOGUE

- Have you ever seen the movie *Victor/Victoria?* It's one of my favorites.
- No, but I heard that it was very funny. Where did you see it?
- Last November I visited my cousin Valerie, and we watched it on her video cassette recorder.
- I think I remember your cousin. She's a vibrant and vivacious woman, isn't she?
- Yes, she lives in Vienna, Virginia now. She used to live in Venezuela, but she moved a few years ago.
- What does she do for a living?
- She's a very clever writer; she writes advertisements for such products as overcoats, shaving cream, and several different types of vinegar.
- That sounds difficult. She must be an above-average writer.

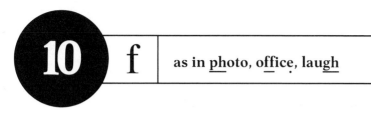

10 **f** | as in <u>ph</u>oto, o<u>ff</u>ice, lau<u>gh</u>

I. PRONUNCIATION

To make this sound, touch your lower lip with your upper front teeth and blow out voicelessly. (The production of this sound is similar to that of [v], except that [f] is voiceless.)

for	offer	enough
flag	affect	leaf
flat	fifty	loaf
favor	often	roof
photograph	defend	tough
phrase	nephew	wolf

II. COMPARISON

Practice these contrasting sounds.

have	half		free	three
save	safe		fought	thought
prove	proof		fan	than
leave	leaf		fat	that

III. REPETITION

1. He followed his father's teaching faithfully.
2. You need have no fear of his failing to fulfill his promise.
3. A fire broke out on the fifth floor.
4. A heavy February frost followed the unusually fair weather.

5. Please feel free to correct my pronunciation faults.
6. We all laughed when Fred, who was so fat, fell off the fence.
7. Philip refused to accept his defeat as final.
8. I'll be free between four and five o'clock.

IV. PHRASING AND INTONATION

a. Blend together the words in each of these phrases or sentences to form a single unit—that is, pronounce each phrase as though it were a single word. Also stress the accented syllable strongly, obscuring the vowels in the remaining syllables.

a pretty párasol	Bill and Cathy Táylor	too láte
a frequent vísitor	He's afraid of fíre.	He's góne.

b. The teacher reads each of the following sentences in a normal manner, giving some slight emphasis to phrasing and intonation. Students repeat after teacher. Teacher repeats after students.

1. (Teacher)   How has Faye been feeling lately?

   (Students) How has Faye been feeling lately?
   (Teacher)   How has Faye been feeling lately?

2. (Teacher)   Is it true that the weather affects one's health?

   (Students) Is it true that the weather affects one's health?
   (Teacher)   Is it true that the weather affects one's health?

3. (Teacher)   Florence and I have been friends for years.

   (Students) Florence and I have been friends for years.
   (Teacher)   Florence and I have been friends for years.

Teachers and students continue in exactly the same manner with these sentences: Teacher reads, students repeat, teacher repeats.

4. The fountain at Verdi often overflows.
5. The climate of Florida is warmer than that of California.
6. Why is Frances so afraid of fire?
7. She was burned badly in a fire when she was five years old.
8. We found the future tense far easier to learn than the past tense.
9. The first game finished at four o'clock.
10. Fred will be free after five o'clock.

V. REVIEW DIALOGUE

- Hi, Phyllis, this is Fred. How are you feeling today?
- Much better, Fred. I've finally finished all my exams. I took my last final this morning.
- How did you fare?
- I think I passed all of them, but I may have failed French. Old Professor Fouchet is a tough grader. He's fair, but he takes off points for the slightest error.
- What about your cough? Is that better?
- Yes. I had a rough night, but my roommate made me take some cough medicine, and now I feel fine. In fact, I was considering going in to Philadelphia this afternoon. Would you like to go?
- Sure. I'll be over after my last class. How does five o'clock sound?
- Fine. I'll see you then, Fred.

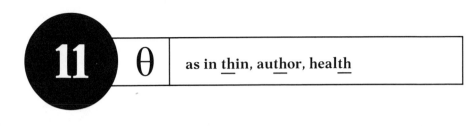

11 θ | as in <u>th</u>in, au<u>th</u>or, heal<u>th</u>

I. PRONUNCIATION

To make this sound, place the tip of your tongue between the cutting edges of your front teeth; then blow out voicelessly.

thin	method	both
thick	author	birth
thing	wealthy	earth
Thursday	nothing	growth
thank	something	health
theater	birthday	breath

II. COMPARISON

Practice these contrasting sounds.

thank	tank	thank	sank
thin	tin	thin	sin
through	true	thing	sing
thought	taught	thumb	some
with	wit	myth	miss
both	boat	mouth	mouse

III. REPETITION

1. Ethel's birthday comes this month.
2. How much is three times three? Three times thirteen?
3. Thursday is the fifteenth of the month.

4. Thirty thousand soldiers marched through the city streets.
5. Thelma was naturally thankful for the gift of three thousand dollars.
6. She thinks and talks of nothing but the theater.
7. I am through with the thread and thimble now.
8. Our theater tickets were for Thursday, the thirteenth.

IV. PHRASING AND INTONATION

a. Blend together the words in each of these phrases to form a single unit—that is, pronounce each phrase as though it were a single word. Also stress the accented syllable strongly, obscuring the vowels in the remaining syllables.

three times threé   through thick and thín   a wealthy aúthor
health is weálth   to have good heálth   to think of sómething
the same páth

b. The teacher reads each of the following sentences in a normal manner, giving some slight emphasis to phrasing and intonation. Students repeat after teacher. Teacher repeats after students.

1. (Teacher)   The author of the story is Theodore Plath.

    (Students)   The author of the story is Theodore Plath.
    (Teacher)   The author of the story is Theodore Plath.

2. (Teacher)   Has Thelma been healthy this month?

    (Students)   Has Thelma been healthy this month?
    (Teacher)   Has Thelma been healthy this month?

3. (Teacher)   Where did Ethel put the Thermos bottle?

    (Students)   Where did Ethel put the Thermos bottle?
    (Teacher)   Where did Ethel put the Thermos bottle?

Teacher and students continue in exactly the same manner with these sentences: Teacher reads, students repeat, teacher repeats.

4. He threw a thunderbolt from his throne.
5. Is Arthur in better health now?
6. Yes, but three days ago, on Thursday, I thought he was getting a thyroid infection.
7. Who is the author of the novel *The Good Earth?*
8. Don't you think you should thank Arthur for the present he gave you?
9. We think we will travel through Europe this summer.
10. Anything worth doing is worth doing thoroughly.

V. REVIEW DIALOGUE

- Bertha has invited us to go to the theater with her on the thirtieth of this month.
- Which theater is it, the one on South Third Street or the one on North Twentieth Street?
- The one on South Third. It's a detective story based on the old *Thin Man* series. I think you'll enjoy it.
- I thought we were going to visit that health spa in Fort Worth on the thirtieth.
- Thanks for reminding me. I don't want anything to prevent us from going to that health program.
- I'll call Bertha and thank her for her thoughtfulness, but I'll tell her we can't go.

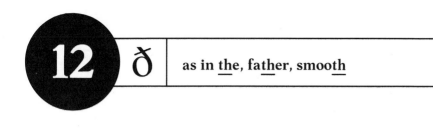

12 ð as in <u>th</u>e, fa<u>th</u>er, smoo<u>th</u>

I. PRONUNCIATION

To make this sound, place your tongue between the cutting edges of your front teeth and blow out a voiced sound. The difference between this sound and [θ] is that this sound is voiced.

the	mother	leather
there	brother	bother
this	neither	wither
that	further	bathe
these	whether	smooth
those	father	breathe

II. COMPARISON

Practice these contrasting sounds.

they	day	that	sat
their	dare	these	seize
though	dough	those	sews
than	Dan	they've	save
breathe	breed	thy	thigh
clothe	close	teethe	teeth

III. REPETITION

1. I didn't know whether he was your father or your brother.
2. It was difficult for them to breathe in such cold weather.

3. There is little good leather on the market now.
4. There is another path farther ahead.
5. Although they were lost, neither one was frightened.
6. My brother would rather sleep than eat.
7. You can choose either one or the other.
8. Neither of them noticed that the other was getting tired.

IV. PHRASING AND INTONATION

a. Blend together the words in each of these phrases or sentences to form a single unit—that is, pronounce each phrase as though it were a single word. Also stress the accented syllable strongly, obscuring the vowels in the remaining syllables.

Why hésitate?	at thát time	either one or twó
Don't bóther them.	expréss line	either pink or blúe

b. The teacher reads each of the following sentences in a normal manner, giving some slight emphasis to phrasing and intonation. Students repeat after teacher. Teacher repeats after students.

1. (Teacher) Which tie shall I wear, this one or that one?

   (Students) Which tie shall I wear, this one or that one?
   (Teacher) Which tie shall I wear, this one or that one?

2. (Teacher) I don't like either one of them.

   (Students) I don't like either one of them.
   (Teacher) I don't like either one of them.

3. (Teacher) Have you seen my brother anywhere?

   (Students) Have you seen my brother anywhere?
   (Teacher) Have you seen my brother anywhere?

Teacher and students continue in exactly the same manner with these sentences: Teacher reads, students repeat, teacher repeats.

4. To whom does that leather bag belong?
5. Would you rather have this one or that?
6. Is that Frank's brother with his father?
7. Where are your mother and father now?
8. This is the night they always go to the theater.
9. I'd rather discuss this matter at another time.
10. They knew that there was no other path out of the woods.

V. REVIEW DIALOGUE

- Were the two of you already together when your brother arrived?
- Yes, but we didn't expect him, you know. He hadn't bothered to get in touch with either of us.
- So neither your mother nor your father knew he was coming?
- Right. They were so surprised, they were speechless. As they described it, "We were rather at a loss for words."
- Was it a happy gathering, nonetheless?
- Oh, yes. We all hugged each other, and then my brother said he was getting tired of the northern climate. He was tired of such cold weather, so he was thinking of moving to a southern state.
- It was another surprise in a day full of them!

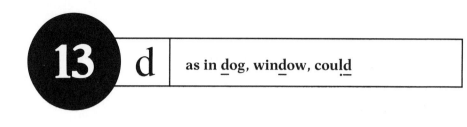

I. PRONUNCIATION

To make this sound, touch the tip of your tongue to the gum ridge behind your upper front teeth. Be careful not to touch your teeth; then blow your tongue away from the ridge sharply, making a voiced sound.

day	candy	bed
dog	children	could
die	today	find
door	ready	good
dress	under	had
down	window	hand
dad	garden	heard

II. COMPARISON

Practice these contrasting sounds.

seed	seethe	dime	time
D	thee	die	tie
fodder	father	down	town

III. REPETITION

1. Today we hid some candy under the tree in the garden.
2. The name of the druggist is Dudley Davis.
3. I doubt whether he would dare to do such a thing.

4. The child hid under the bed.
5. We made good time on our drive to Detroit.
6. David finally paid the ten dollars he owed me.
7. The dean talked with Doris about her low grades.
8. That child seldom does what he is told.

IV. PHRASING AND INTONATION

a. Blend together the words in each of these phrases or sentences to form a single unit—that is, pronounce each phrase as though it were a single word. Also stress the accented syllable strongly, obscuring the vowels in the remaining syllables.

from door to do′or	ópera star	Don't téll him about it.
a bright red dréss	Stáy a while.	Tell Bétty to do it.
mother and dád	cándy cane	Let Álice accept it.

b. The teacher reads each of the following sentences in a normal manner, giving some slight emphasis to phrasing and intonation. Students repeat after teacher. Teacher repeats after students.

1. (Teacher) Did you hear that loud sound?

   (Students) Did you hear that loud sound?
   (Teacher)   Did you hear that loud sound?

2. (Teacher) Yes, it came from the garden.

   (Students) Yes, it came from the garden.
   (Teacher)   Yes, it came from the garden.

3. (Teacher) What did you do all day yesterday?

   (Students) What did you do all day yesterday?
   (Teacher)   What did you do all day yesterday?

Teacher and students continue in exactly the same manner with these sentences: Teacher reads, students repeat, teacher repeats.

4. Do both children always drink their milk?
5. Sometimes they do, and sometimes they don't.
6. What did Donald say about his trip?
7. He didn't mention a word about it.
8. Did you read Dora's letter?
9. You went for a long drive today, didn't you?
10. Yes, we got up at dawn to do it.

V. PRONUNCIATION OF TERMINAL *ed*

The ending *ed*, when added to any regular verb to form the simple past tense, is pronounced as follows:

1. It is pronounced as a separate syllable [ɪd] if the verb ends in *t* or *d*.

    wait   waited (pronounced *wait ed* [wétɪd])
    want   wanted (pronounced *want ed* [wántɪd])

2. It is pronounced [t] if the verb ends in any voiceless sound (except *t*).

    ask   asked (pronounced *asked* [æskt])
    wash   washed (pronounced *washed* [wɑʃt])

3. It is pronounced [d] if the verb ends in any voiced sound (except *d*).

    play   played (pronounced *played* [pled])
    turn   turned (pronounced *turned* [tɝnd])

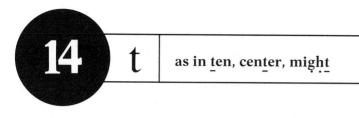

I. PRONUNCIATION

To make this sound, touch the tip of your tongue to the gum ridge behind your upper front teeth. Be careful not to touch your teeth; then blow your tongue away from the ridge sharply and voicelessly.

tea	ashtray	shirt
ten	retain	but
to	partake	eat
teach	sister	get
table	pretend	foot
tell	sustain	fast

II. COMPARISON

Practice these contrasting sounds.

to	do	feet	feed
tore	door	bet	bed
toe	dough	bat	bad
tip	dip	debt	dead

III. REPETITION

1. The attack began at ten o'clock and continued until dawn.
2. We had great difficulty in locating the origin of the trouble.
3. Tom wrote the letter immediately.

4. The heat within the tent was so great that no one could sleep.
5. The child is too young to tell time.
6. We tried several times to reach him by telephone.
7. The tire had been punctured by a small tack.
8. The cat sat calmly on the top step.

IV. PHRASING AND INTONATION

a. Blend together the words in each of these phrases or sentences to form a single unit—that is, pronounce each phrase as though it were a single word. Also stress the accented syllable strongly, obscuring the vowels in the remaining syllables.

little by líttle	go for cóffee	Watch out for tráffic jams.
a glass of wáter	bread and bútter	go to the récord shop
to write a létter	lazy stúdents	more than he bárgained for

b. The teacher reads each of the following sentences in a normal manner, giving some slight emphasis to phrasing and intonation. Students repeat after teacher. Teacher repeats after students.

1. (Teacher) What's the matter with Tom today?

   (Students) What's the matter with Tom today?
   (Teacher) What's the matter with Tom today?

2. (Teacher) I haven't the faintest idea.

   (Students) I haven't the faintest idea.
   (Teacher) I haven't the faintest idea.

3. (Teacher) Haven't you written to your aunt yet?

   (Students) Haven't you written to your aunt yet?
   (Teacher) Haven't you written to your aunt yet?

Teacher and students continue in exactly the same manner with these sentences: Teacher reads, students repeat, teacher repeats.

4. I really hate to write letters.
5. How much is two times two? Ten times ten?
6. Where is your little sister?
7. She's outside playing with the kitten.
8. Night after night, they played their radio until almost midnight.
9. Tina and Tony went into the city last Saturday.
10. That was the time we took Tara to the train station.

V. TERMINAL *ed* PRONUNCIATION PRACTICE

separate syllable [ɪd]	*ed* pronounced [t]	*ed* pronounced [d]
wanted	dressed	lived
handed	liked	mailed
attended	thanked	believed
affected	decreased	contained
added	jumped	cleaned
accepted	noticed	learned
ended	walked	dialed
needed	stopped	explained
decided	worked	followed
excited	picked	imagined
interested	placed	loved

15 | **1** | as in <u>l</u>ady, fo<u>ll</u>ow, we<u>ll</u>

I. PRONUNCIATION

To make this sound, touch the tip of your tongue to the gum ridge behind your upper front teeth. Keep the middle of your tongue high and the sides relaxed; then let a voiced breath come over the sides.

left	believe	all
leave	hello	call
little	only	girl
life	belong	shall
long	follow	will
like	silent	tell
lip	careless	well

II. COMPARISON

Practice these contrasting sounds.

long	wrong	climb	crime	file	fire
light	right	pull	purr	call	car
list	wrist	mall	mar	bill	beer
late	rate	tall	tore	stole	store

III. REPETITION

1. His illness kept him from completing the work.
2. The law was repealed by the legislature.

3. Her life seemed to be a series of long illnesses.
4. He who laughs last laughs best.
5. Della's umbrella lay floating in the lake.
6. The last line of the poem caused a good deal of laughter.
7. The leaves turn yellow in early autumn.
8. Lake Superior is the largest of the Great Lakes.

IV. PHRASING AND INTONATION

a. Blend together the words in each of these phrases or sentences to form a single unit—that is, pronounce each phrase as though it were a single word. Also stress the accented syllable strongly, obscuring the vowels in the remaining syllables.

red Vólvos	All is wéll.	Will you wáit?
the néxt time	late at níght	Is it tíme?
the drý one	to live wéll	Did he leáve?

b. The teacher reads each of the following sentences in a normal manner, giving some slight emphasis to phrasing and intonation. Students repeat after teacher. Teacher repeats after students.

1. (Teacher)   Would you like to look at the lake?

   (Students) Would you like to look at the lake?
   (Teacher)   Would you like to look at the lake?

2. (Teacher)   I'd like very much to see the lake.

   (Students) I'd like very much to see the lake.
   (Teacher)   I'd like very much to see the lake.

3. (Teacher)   Where shall we meet for lunch?

   (Students) Where shall we meet for lunch?
   (Teacher)   Where shall we meet for lunch?

Teacher and students continue in exactly the same manner with these sentences: Teacher reads, students repeat, teacher repeats.

4. Let's meet in front of Lane's Department Store.
5. A little boy just fell into the lake.
6. Will it take long to deliver this merchandise?
7. Laura left a little after eleven.
8. Is Della telling us the truth or telling a lie?
9. Do those letters belong to you?
10. No, they all belong to Louise.

V. REVIEW DIALOGUE

- Stella's cold is a little worse. I think we should call Dr. Mullen, don't you Leslie?
- Well, Bill, I guess you're right. She's had chills all morning.
- It's clear to me that she doesn't feel well.
- Instead of calling, let's just take her over to the clinic. Perhaps they'll be able to see her right away.
- But if we call Dr. Mullen, she may be able to tell us what to do over the telephone. We'll save a trip outside in this cold weather.
- Good thinking. I'll call her while you take this hot tea with lemon in to Stella. Let's hope the doctor is not out playing golf.

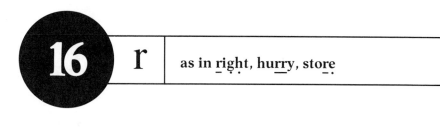

16 r   as in right, hurry, store

I. PRONUNCIATION

To make this sound, raise your tongue and curl it toward the hard palate without letting it touch the palate or move while you blow out a voiced breath.

room	proud	very	car
run	try	direction	purr
red	tree	marry	her
ride	drive	story	fear
Robert	pretty	correct	choir
rat	price	favorite	power
			fire

II. COMPARISON

Practice these contrasting sounds.

ride	wide	rate	wait	par	paw
read	weed	run	won	cart	caught
red	wed	rest	west	sore	sew
rent	went	ring	wing	tore	toll

III. REPETITION

1. The river rose several inches as a result of the rain.
2. The rain ruined all our pretty flowers.

3. We were required to take both an oral and a written examination.
4. It has been over a year since he first began work on the book.
5. Ruth hurt her right wrist when she fell.
6. In some languages, one reads from right to left rather than from left to right.
7. The view of the river from here is perfect.
8. Every afternoon, Richard and Rose go roller-skating in Central Park.

IV. PHRASING AND INTONATION

a. Blend together the words in each of these phrases or sentences to form a single unit—that is, pronounce each phrase as though it were a single word. Also stress the accented syllable strongly, obscuring the vowels in the remaining syllables.

ready to lánd	to write a létter	play cárds
He likes to dríve.	to need more práctice	blue cheése
more than a yeár	a lot of léttuce	clean hánds

b. The teacher reads each of the following sentences in a normal manner, giving some slight emphasis to phrasing and intonation. Students repeat after teacher. Teacher repeats after students.

1. (Teacher) When is Richard's birthday?

   (Students) When is Richard's birthday?
   (Teacher) When is Richard's birthday?

2. (Teacher) His birthday is the twenty-third of April.

   (Students) His birthday is the twenty-third of April.
   (Teacher) His birthday is the twenty-third of April.

3. (Teacher) Do you practice these drills on pronunciation?

(Students)   Do you practice these drills on pronunciation?
(Teacher)   Do you practice these drills on pronunciation?

Teacher and students continue in exactly the same manner with these sentences: Teacher reads, students repeat, teacher repeats.

4. I practice them whenever I have time.
5. What would you like for breakfast?
6. I'll have orange juice, cereal, and coffee, please.
7. We drove the entire length of Riverside Drive.
8. That's a very pretty dress Rose is wearing.
9. All his answers to the professor's questions were wrong.
10. It has been raining hard all morning.

V. REVIEW DIALOGUE

- Were you surprised when you heard that Ray was running for the House of Representatives?
- No, I rather expected it. After he became president of his firm, it was more and more apparent that he wanted to enter politics.
- He started as a stockbroker, didn't he?
- Yes. In fact, he was a runner in a Wall Street brokerage house for several years, but he worked very hard and eventually was promoted.
- I remember. Back in those days, our apartments were near each other. We were neighbors. I suppose if he wins, he'll move to Washington.
- Actually, he'll probably move to a suburb of Washington, in Maryland or Virginia.

17 S as in <u>c</u>ity, per<u>s</u>on, ri<u>ce</u>

I. PRONUNCIATION

To make this sound, touch the sides of your tongue to the tooth ridge and make a hissing, voiceless sound over the curved middle of your tongue.

seat	listen	pass
seldom	lesson	face
same	office	dress
sell	sister	house
saw	cost	lace
smoke	assist	mass

II. COMPARISON

Practice these contrasting sounds.

loose	lose	sing	thing
price	prize	sank	thank
peace	peas	sin	thin
place	plays	sick	thick

III. REPETITION

1. We passed several small ships at sea.
2. She sent us six presents this past Christmas.
3. This office saved a considerable sum of money over the last fiscal year.

4. The cemetery is close to our house.
5. Did you go to that special sale at the supermarket?
6. Yesterday was my sister's first wedding anniversary.
7. Sam went to the post office to buy some stamps.
8. Seawater is too salty to drink.

IV. PHRASING AND INTONATION

a. Blend together the words in each of these phrases or sentences to form a single unit—that is, pronounce each phrase as though it were a single word. Also stress the accented syllable strongly, obscuring the vowels in the remaining syllables.

a front seát	She's very síck.	no hópe for him
on the roóf	He passed the coúrse.	less wórk to do
a nice dáy	What a surpríse!	ten tímes as much

b. The teacher reads each of the following sentences in a normal manner, giving some slight emphasis to phrasing and intonation. Students repeat after teacher. Teacher repeats after students.

1. (Teacher) How many students are there in your class?

   (Students) How many students are there in your class?
   (Teacher) How many students are there in your class?

2. (Teacher) There are ten boys and eight girls in the class.

   (Students) There are ten boys and eight girls in the class.
   (Teacher) There are ten boys and eight girls in the class.

3. (Teacher) Have you ever traveled through the South?

   (Students) Have you ever traveled through the South?
   (Teacher) Have you ever traveled through the South?

Teacher and students continue in exactly the same manner with these sentences: Teacher reads, students repeat, teacher repeats.

4. I once took a short trip to South Carolina.
5. We see Sam and Sarah at least twice a week.
6. Ice-skating is not popular in Mississippi.
7. The professor talks too fast for us.
8. I got two good seats in the seventh row for Saturday night.

V. PRONUNCIATION OF FINAL *s*

An *s* may appear at the end of a word because of its spelling *(pass, his)* or because it is a contracted form of *is* or *has (she is – she's, it has – it's)*. An *s* is added to the end of a noun to form its plural *(book – books)* and to the end of a verb to form its third person singular, present tense *(think – she thinks)*. An *s* is also added to the end of a noun, with an apostrophe, in order to show possession *(the girl – the girl's desk)*. The final *s* is pronounced [s] when it follows an unvoiced sound; it is pronounced [z] when it follows a voiced sound.

Final s Pronounced [s]　　　　　　　　*Final s Pronounced* [z]

(Nouns)

books	doctors	pears
maps	pencils	days
clocks	teachers	hands
hats	trains	windows
months	dogs	

(Verbs)

eats	comes
takes	goes
speaks	leaves
thanks	arrives

(Contractions)

what's	he's
that's	she's
it's	there's

(Possessive Form)

Mr. *Smith's* friend	*Henry's* friend
the *student's* book	the *dog's* tail
the *cat's* tail	the *boy's* room

18 Z | as in zoo, easy, lose

I. PRONUNCIATION

To make this sound, touch the sides of your tongue to the tooth ridge and make a buzzing sound over the curved middle of your tongue.

zone	razor	as
zoo	result	bags
zebra	lazy	learns
zero	museum	Ms. [mɪz]
zinc	dizzy	nose
Zelda	loser	buzz
xylophone	daisy	rise

II. COMPARISON

Practice these contrasting sounds.

price	prize	Sue	zoo	rice	rise
ice	eyes	sink	zinc	facing	fazing
pace	pays	see	Z	lacy	lazy
loose	lose	bus	buzz	face	phase

III. REPETITION

1. Excuse me, please. I have a cold, so I am sneezing.
2. She always opens the door with these keys.

3. I have two sisters and three brothers.
4. We teased our little cousin unreasonably.
5. Did you think your zoology quiz was easy or difficult?
6. My father sent my mother a dozen roses on their anniversary.
7. The newspaper article criticized the music in that movie.
8. The bees buzzed busily around the flowers.

IV. PHRASING AND INTONATION

a. Blend together the words in each of these phrases or sentences to form a single unit—that is, pronounce each phrase as though it were a single word. Also stress the accented syllable strongly, obscuring the vowels in the remaining syllables.

Mr. Péterson	It's all made of wíre.	a sad cómment
clean the táble top	Why not buy the tíre?	a warm wínter
warn the pássengers	I can't find the fíle.	a good dáncer

b. The teacher reads each of the following sentences in a normal manner, giving some slight emphasis to phrasing and intonation. Students repeat after teacher. Teacher repeats after students.

1. (Teacher)   Does Hazel study English in your class?

   (Students) Does Hazel study English in your class?
   (Teacher)   Does Hazel study English in your class?

2. (Teacher)   No, Hazel studies in Mary's class.

   (Students) No, Hazel studies in Mary's class.
   (Teacher)   No, Hazel studies in Mary's class.

3. (Teacher)   Why didn't you call a physician?

   (Students) Why didn't you call a physician?
   (Teacher)   Why didn't you call a physician?

Teacher and students continue in exactly the same manner with these sentences: Teacher reads, students repeat, teacher repeats.

4. Do you often visit the zoo?
5. Their favorite type of music is jazz.
6. What size gloves does Daisy wear?
7. On Tuesday, we visited our cousin in Missouri.
8. It's more than a thousand miles from here to Arizona.
9. "This is crazy," she said as she changed the calendar from Wednesday to Thursday.
10. It says in this booklet that going into the business of selling shoes isn't easy.

V. PRONUNCIATION OF FINAL *es*

Nouns that end in *s, z, ch, sh, tch,* or *x* form their plurals by adding *es.* Similarly, verbs that end in these letters form their third person singular, present tense by adding *es.* This *es* is always pronounced as a separate syllable, [ɪz] or [əz].

Nouns		*Verbs*	
class	classes	kiss	kisses
bus	buses	pass	passes
buzz	buzzes	fizz	fizzes
beach	beaches	punch	punches
wish	wishes	rush	rushes
match	matches	watch	watches
ax	axes	tax	taxes

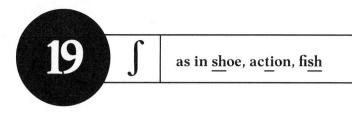

19 ∫   as in <u>sh</u>oe, ac<u>ti</u>on, fi<u>sh</u>

I. PRONUNCIATION

To make this sound, push out your lips a little, and place the tip of your tongue close to the upper gum ridge but not touching it. Curve your tongue with the sides higher than the middle, and make a voiceless "shh" sound.

shop	fashion	wish
share	ocean	wash
she	election	push
shall	delicious	rush
shoulder	pressure	Irish
short	bushel	dish
sheet	depression	cash

II. COMPARISON

Practice these contrasting sounds.

short	sort	sheep	cheap	mash	match
sheet	seat	shin	chin	wish	witch
shock	sock	share	chair	mush	much
shell	sell	shop	chop	cash	catch

III. REPETITION

1. I had no wish to make an issue of the matter.
2. The sheep pushed through the open gate and spread quickly along the shore of the lake.

3. The report clearly showed the position of the ships before the battle.
4. Pushing roughly past us, the man rushed into the shop.
5. She spent her vacation at the seashore.
6. The shelves of the shop were full of old dishes.
7. Mr. Shaw always shines his own shoes.
8. Shirley hurt her shoulder when she fell.

IV. PHRASING AND INTONATION

a. Blend together the words in each of these phrases or sentences to form a single unit—that is, pronounce each phrase as though it were a single word. Also stress the accented syllable strongly, obscuring the vowels in the remaining syllables.

a táxpayer	big and hard to cáre for	Speak úp if you want some.
a wásh basin	all the heavy hárdware	Who cáres if it's ugly?
on tóp of	soft and gentle láther	Just óne will do nicely.

b. The teacher reads each of the following sentences in a normal manner, giving some slight emphasis to phrasing and intonation. Students repeat after teacher. Teacher repeats after students.

1. (Teacher) Did you go shopping yesterday?

   (Students) Did you go shopping yesterday?
   (Teacher) Did you go shopping yesterday?

2. (Teacher) Yes, but many of the shops were closed.

   (Students) Yes, but many of the shops were closed.
   (Teacher) Yes, but many of the shops were closed.

3. (Teacher) How often does he shine his shoes?

   (Students) How often does he shine his shoes?
   (Teacher) How often does he shine his shoes?

Teacher and students continue in exactly the same manner with these sentences: Teacher reads, students repeat, teacher repeats.

4. I know that he doesn't shine them as often as he should.
5. Why did Sherry say she wished he would lose the election?
6. When I dropped the dishes, there was a loud crash.
7. The shelves in the shop were filled with shaving gear.
8. We should finish this work before we take our examination.
9. There were special instructions showing us how to install the shower.
10. I wish she would push me all the time.

V. REVIEW DIALOGUE

- Sheldon and I are going on vacation next month, but we haven't decided where we're going yet.
- Where do you wish you were going, Shirley?
- I'd like to go to the seashore. I love to fish and watch the ships and splash around in the ocean.
- Sheldon probably wants to go to Chicago, doesn't he?
- He sure does. He thinks we should head in the direction of Chicago and stop off in the Shenandoah Valley for a few days. He even has a map of the nation on our wall showing what our route would be.
- Good luck on resolving your problem. Sherman and I are going to Charlotte, North Carolina, this year. We're going to visit his sister who's a cashier in a specialty shop there.

I. PRONUNCIATION

To make this sound, push out your lips a little, and place the tip of your tongue close to the upper gum ridge but not touching it. Curve your tongue with the sides higher than the middle, and make a buzzing sound.

pleasure	treasure	casual
leisure	garage	rouge
decision	usual	confusion
collision	conclusion	persuasion
measure	explosion	provision
invasion	division	excursion

II. COMPARISON

Many students confuse the sound [ʒ] with the sound in the previous unit, [ʃ]. To guard against this tendency, pronounce [ʒ] with strong voicing.

For special practice with this sound, pronounce the following nonsense syllables, laying strong stress on the voiced quality of the first two letters.

zha [ʒɑ]	zhi [ʒi]	zho [ʒo]	zhu [ʒu]
zha	zhi	zho	zhu
zha	zhi	zho	zhu

III. REPETITION

1. The explosion was unusually forceful; it completely destroyed the garage.

2. He's just a casual acquaintance whom I occasionally run into on the street.
3. I've reached the conclusion that his poor vision caused the collision.
4. Her rouge offset her beige blouse perfectly.
5. In his leisure time, he attempted a complete revision of the plans.
6. We usually leave our car in a garage on Tenth Street.
7. The collision of the two trains caused great confusion.
8. The decision to begin the invasion at dawn was a wise one.

IV. PHRASING AND INTONATION

a. Blend together the words in each of these phrases to form a single unit—that is, pronounce each phrase as though it were a single word. Also stress the accented syllable strongly, obscuring the vowels in the remaining syllables.

an important decísion	too much léisure time	some féathers
an unusual pérson	extra pénalty	the túnnel
a casual acquáintance	golden mémory	too lázy

b. The teacher reads each of the following sentences in a normal manner, giving some slight emphasis to phrasing and intonation. Students repeat after teacher. Teacher repeats after students.

1. (Teacher) Where did the collision take place?

   (Students) Where did the collision take place?
   (Teacher) Where did the collision take place?

2. (Teacher) It took place in front of the Bolton Building.

   (Students) It took place in front of the Bolton Building.
   (Teacher) It took place in front of the Bolton Building.

3. (Teacher) Do you enjoy going on excursions?

(Students)   Do you enjoy going on excursions?
(Teacher)   Do you enjoy going on excursions?

Teacher and students continue in exactly the same manner with these sentences: Teacher reads, students repeat, teacher repeats.

4. Frankly, I have never gone anywhere on an excursion.
5. What does Mr. Mosher do with all his leisure time?
6. He has a workshop in his garage where he usually spends a lot of time.
7. What was the cause of the explosion?
8. The police have not yet reached a decision in the matter.
9. Ask the garage mechanic to measure the oil.
10. I came to the conclusion that I had forgotten to do my long division problems for homework.

V. HOMONYMS

Pronounce these pairs of homonyms and distinguish their meanings.

their	there	knight	night	cent	scent
weight	wait	know	no	scene	seen
threw	through	cell	sell	forth	fourth
knew	new	cellar	seller	die	dye
waist	waste	sail	sale	flour	flower
way	weigh	sees	seize	road	rode
weak	week	berth	birth	right	write
wood	would	heal	heel	knead	need

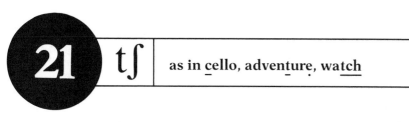

I. PRONUNCIATION

To make this sound, push your lips out a little and raise your tongue to the upper gum ridge; then voicelessly glide the sounds [t] and [ʃ] together.

chair	actual	reach
chief	capture	teach
chess	butcher	couch
choice	feature	approach
choose	natural	lunch
cheap	ancient	march

II. COMPARISON

Practice these contrasting sounds.

chew	shoe	choke	joke	watch	wash
chin	shin	cheap	jeep	match	mash
cheap	sheep	chin	gin	march	marsh
cheat	sheet	choice	Joyce	ditch	dish

III. REPETITION

1. Chester chose a rich-looking gold watch as his present.
2. They checked the ancient Chinese tomb.
3. We have no choice except to change our plans.

4. After lunch, we watched a tennis match between Charles and Jim.
5. Mr. Chase is going to teach me how to play chess.
6. The child reached up and touched the chair.
7. We have a cherry tree and a peach tree in our back yard.
8. Don't count your chickens before they are hatched.

IV. PHRASING AND INTONATION

a. Blend together the words in each of these phrases or sentences to form a single unit—that is, pronounce each phrase as though it were a single word. Also stress the accented syllable strongly, obscuring the vowels in the remaining syllables.

to catch a físh	Where's the chéckroom?	take a trip to
right after lúnch	have a heádache	Náples
to go to chúrch	find the ánswer	up and down the highway
		Joe and Esther Pérkins

b. The teacher reads each of the following sentences in a normal manner, giving some slight emphasis to phrasing and intonation. Students repeat after teacher. Teacher repeats after students.

1. (Teacher) How often do they go to church?

   (Students) How often do they go to church?
   (Teacher) How often do they go to church?

2. (Teacher) They go to church each Sunday.

   (Students) They go to church each Sunday.
   (Teacher) They go to church each Sunday.

3. (Teacher) Do you know how to play chess?

(Students)   Do you know how to play chess?
(Teacher)   Do you know how to play chess?

Teacher and students continue in exactly the same manner with these sentences: Teacher reads, students repeat, teacher repeats.

4.   Yes, but I don't play chess very well.
5.   What is the price of these handkerchiefs?
6.   These handkerchiefs cost one dollar each.
7.   Does your new watch keep good time?
8.   No, it's a cheap watch and does not run too well.
9.   Who is your favorite teacher?
10.   My favorite teacher is Miss Chapman.

V. REVIEW DIALOGUE

- Let's turn on the TV. I'd like to watch an old Charlie Chan movie.
- Charlie Chan? Isn't he that fictional Chinese detective?
- Yes. My teacher says he was famous during the 1940s and 1950s. In his motion pictures, he used to capture criminals with the help of his sons. It might be fun.
- O.K. Let's have sandwiches while we watch; I'll make them. Would you like a cheese sandwich or a chicken sandwich? We also have some potato chips.
- Actually, I'm not hungry; I had a late lunch, but you go ahead. I'll find the right channel and set up our chairs for watching.
- Thanks.

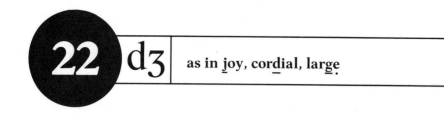

I. PRONUNCIATION

To make this sound, touch the tip of your tongue to the upper gum ridge and push your lips out a little. Then glide the sounds [d] and [ʒ] together with voicing.

judge	soldier	wage
jail	subject	damage
joke	enjoy	image
joy	manager	page
jewel	major	edge
jaw	urgent	stage
G	magic	judge

II. COMPARISON

Practice these contrasting sounds.

joke	choke	jet	yet	edge	etch
jeep	cheap	jot	yacht	badge	batch
gin	chin	jail	Yale	Madge	match
jeer	cheer	Jess	yes	age	H

III. REPETITION

1. The judge found her jewels behind a jar of orange juice.
2. Joe Jeffreys has been appointed manager of the new travel agency.

3. Apparently, no one enjoyed the joke as much as Joanne herself.
4. General Jackson marched his Confederate soldiers into Georgia.
5. My cookbook has dozens of pages on the subject of steaming vegetables.
6. Both passengers were injured when the carriage overturned.
7. John enjoyed watching the Japanese jugglers.
8. The village bridge was badly damaged by the heavy rains.

IV. PHRASING AND INTONATION

a. Blend together the words in each of these phrases or sentences to form a single unit—that is, pronounce each phrase as though it were a single word. Also stress the accented syllable strongly, obscuring the vowels in the remaining syllables.

buy a dozen éggs	What síze did he try on?	ápple tree
What a noisy chíld!	a saúsage factory	éngine part
We enjoyed the shów.	a trável agency	ténnis pro

b. The teacher reads each of the following sentences in a normal manner, giving some slight emphasis to phrasing and intonation. Students repeat after teacher. Teacher repeats after students.

1. (Teacher)   What is that strange│noise│I hear?

   (Students)   What is that strange noise I hear?
   (Teacher)   What is that strange noise I hear?

2. (Teacher)   The wind in the trees makes ⌐ many noises.

   (Students)   The wind in the trees makes many noises.

(Teacher)   The wind in the trees makes many noises.

3. (Teacher)   Did you enjoy the concert last night?

(Students)   Did you enjoy the concert last night?
(Teacher)   Did you enjoy the concert last night?

Teacher and students continue in exactly the same manner with these sentences: Teacher reads, students repeat, teacher repeats.

4. Yes, I enjoyed it very much.
5. Do you drink much orange juice?
6. Yes, I drink orange juice every morning for breakfast.
7. Who arranged the flowers in that vase?
8. Julia arranged them. Aren't they lovely?
9. What is your favorite subject at school?
10. Geography has always been my favorite subject.

V. REVIEW DIALOGUE

- Were you born in June or July? I always forget.
- July. In fact, my birthday coincides with the celebration of Jesse James Day in Northfield, Minnesota.
- But I thought you were from Virginia.
- I am, but I just got a package from my aunt, Judge Jennifer Jackson, who lives in Northfield. She always manages to get involved with the Jesse James Day festivities. Last year, she sent me some jams and jellies. Let's see what's in this package.
- A book on practical jokes! What an interesting subject!
- Now I'll be able to play jokes on all my friends.

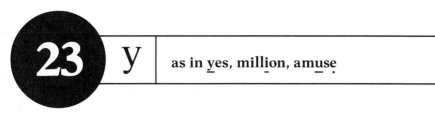

I. PRONUNCIATION

To make this sound, raise your tongue to a high position; then curl the tip down. Do not touch the roof of the mouth with your tongue; then force out a voiced breath.

yes	yawn	amuse
year	use	lawyer
you	genius	Italian
yet	onion	Spaniard
young	beyond	Hawaiian
yesterday	opinion	familiar
excuse	few	loyal

II. COMPARISON

Practice these contrasting sounds.

yet	jet	you	chew
yellow	Jell-O	yes	chess
year	jeer	use	choose
Yale	jail	year	cheer

III. REPETITION

1. My brilliant young traveling companion was named Yolanda.
2. Kirk is a millionaire, even though he is not yet forty.

3. Daniel is a junior in high school. Next year he'll be a senior.
4. Is William a Spaniard or an Italian?
5. Your lawyer seems to be a very young woman.
6. You used that same, old, familiar excuse yesterday and last January, too.
7. Some people call citizens of the United States Yankees.
8. The population of Utah is a little over a million.

IV. PHRASING AND INTONATION

a. Blend together the words in each of these phrases or sentences to form a single unit—that is, pronounce each phrase as though it were a single word. Also stress the accented syllable strongly, obscuring the vowels in the remaining syllables.

the fellow that wón	the wings of a bút-	You're yáwning.
a brilliant young mán	terfly	I'm reády.
the yolk of an égg	the stars in the úni-	all óver
	verse	
	a car like a Cádillac	

b. The teacher reads each of the following sentences in a normal manner, giving some slight emphasis to phrasing and intonation. Students repeat after teacher. Teacher repeats after students.

1. (Teacher) Who is that child in the yellow dress?

   (Students) Who is that child in the yellow dress?
   (Teacher) Who is that child in the yellow dress?

2. (Teacher) Do they still live in Yonkers?

   (Students) Do they still live in Yonkers?
   (Teacher) Do they still live in Yonkers?

3. (Teacher) No, they moved to New York yesterday.

(Students)   No, they moved to New York yesterday.
(Teacher)   No, they moved to New York yesterday.

Teacher and students continue in exactly the same manner with these sentences: Teacher reads, students repeat, teacher repeats.

4. This yellow pencil is yours, not mine.
5. William plans to attend Yale University.
6. To whom does that big yacht belong?
7. It belongs to an official of the Italian government.
8. The yarn which she bought for the sweater was bright yellow.
9. We won't see you again until next year.

V. REVIEW DIALOGUE

- Ms. Young, what's your opinion on the union difficulties?
- Do you mean the management-labor problems at United Industries?
- Yes. You're their lawyer, aren't you?
- Yes. The problem is a familiar one. The union wants more money for its members, while management wants to cut costs. I understand the workers' demands, but I'm loyal to the owners. After all, they pay my salary.
- Yesterday the union negotiator said that his workers would hold out until the new year, that is, until January 1, if they had to. Do you expect the problem to go beyond that date?
- I'm sorry, I don't usually discuss this matter with the press. You'll have to excuse me.

24 | **k** | as in <u>ch</u>ara<u>c</u>ter, Ameri<u>c</u>an, stea<u>k</u>

I. PRONUNCIATION

To make this sound, touch your soft palate with the back part of your tongue; then make a voiceless sound as you quickly break contact.

cat	o'clock	look
can	because	make
call	picture	like
come	American	thank
cool	school	took
cut	escape	walk
queen	instruction	bark
keep	breakfast	check

II. COMPARISON

Practice these contrasting sounds.

coat	goat	rack	rag
cold	gold	back	bag
coast	ghost	duck	dug
come	gum	leak	league

III. REPETITION

1. Carl came home after his vacation.
2. I was weak after the long climb up the cliff.

3. The crowd cheered the king and queen.
4. My cousin Carol lives in Canada, but in October she's moving to Kentucky.
5. The cook baked a delicious cake for Jack's birthday party.
6. The cat is playing with her kittens.
7. I plucked the chicken before six o'clock.
8. You were lucky that the ink didn't stain the carpet.

IV. PHRASING AND INTONATION

a. Blend together the words in each of these phrases or sentences to form a single unit—that is, pronounce each phrase as though it were a single word. Also stress the accented syllable strongly, obscuring the vowels in the remaining syllables.

the last tráin	What a cute kítten!	Thank Káthryn for it.
a clear dáy	The dog is bárking.	It's rúde to shout so.
to work hárd	It's a real beáuty.	Why tálk about it?

b. The teacher reads each of the following sentences in a normal manner, giving some slight emphasis to phrasing and intonation. Students repeat after teacher. Teacher repeats after students.

1. (Teacher)   Can you come at six o'clock?

   (Students)   Can you come at six o'clock?
   (Teacher)   Can you come at six o'clock?

2. (Teacher)   I can, but Carol can't.

   (Students)   I can, but Carol can't.
   (Teacher)   I can, but Carol can't.

3. (Teacher)   What would you like for breakfast?

   (Students)   What would you like for breakfast?
   (Teacher)   What would you like for breakfast?

Teacher and students continue in exactly the same manner with these sentences: Teacher reads, students repeat, teacher repeats.

4. I'd like bacon and eggs, biscuits, and coffee.
5. Will the cat come if you call her name?
6. No, but she'll come if she hears you opening a can of cat food.
7. The quintuplets live in Saskatoon, Saskatchewan.
8. It looks like he can't quit smoking.

V. REVIEW DIALOGUE

- Can your cat do tricks?
- She usually comes when I call her, but you can't make cats do tricks.
- Does she like canned food?
- Yes, but she likes cake and ice cream, too.
- Does she exercise enough?
- Too much. She often breaks things just walking around.
- Does she like to ride in cars?
- No, but she likes to go to the country club with us. Once we're there, she hates to come back.

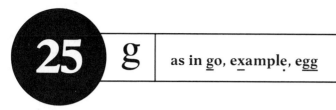

I. PRONUNCIATION

To make this sound, touch your soft palate with the back part of your tongue; then make a voiced sound as you quickly break contact.

good	forget	big
go	forgotten	dog
get	again	egg
girl	ago	leg
give	together	flag
guess	sugar	dig
great	examine	dialogue

II. COMPARISON

Practice these contrasting sounds.

go	Joe	good	could	lug	luck
bag	badge	gay	Kay	gauze	cause
bigger	bicker	ghoul	cool	pig	pick
dog	dodge	game	came	tag	tack

III. REPETITION

1. Greg forgot to study for the English examination.
2. Professor Grant regretted not giving Gwen a better grade.
3. The game began as soon as the fog lifted.

4. Gertrude cut her finger on a piece of glass.
5. The teacher gave both girls good marks.
6. A dog had dug up all the flowers in our carefully planted garden.
7. Grace is going to the game, but Gertrude isn't.
8. They sell good sandwiches in Grey's Drugstore.

IV. PHRASING AND INTONATION

a. Blend together the words in each of these phrases or sentences to form a single unit—that is, pronounce each phrase as though it were a single word. Also stress the accented syllable strongly, obscuring the vowels in the remaining syllables

the youngest són	a néws report	grab a paper nápkin
Try it agáin.	some fóod to eat	go and join the ármy
a paper bág	Take cáre of it.	weak and foolish víctim

b. The teacher reads each of the following sentences in a normal manner, giving some slight emphasis to phrasing and intonation. Students repeat after teacher. Teacher repeats after students.

1. (Teacher) Can you go to the game with us?

   (Students) Can you go to the game with us?
   (Teacher) Can you go to the game with us?

2. (Teacher) No, we'll have to get together another time.

   (Students) No, we'll have to get together another time.
   (Teacher) No, we'll have to get together another time.

3. (Teacher) How did you hurt your finger?

   (Students) How did you hurt your finger?
   (Teacher) How did you hurt your finger?

Teacher and students continue in exactly the same manner with these sentences: Teacher reads, students repeat, teacher repeats.

4. I caught it in the garden gate.
5. Have you done your English grammar exercises yet?
6. Not yet, but I'm going to do them now.
7. How many girls are there in your group?
8. I don't know exactly. About thirty, I guess.
9. What vegetables grow best in your garden?
10. Asparagus grows well; also, green beans.

V. REVIEW DIALOGUE

- I'm going to stop smoking cigars and cigarettes.
- Good for you!
- Yes, I read an article in the August edition of *Good Housekeeping* magazine which finally convinced me.
- When are you going to begin? I mean stop.
- I guess I already have begun. I decided that since I was going to be a guest in your home, I wouldn't smoke while I'm here.
- I think you'll be setting a fine example for your girls, Gladys and Grace. Now, how about some breakfast? Would you like some eggs and grapefruit juice?

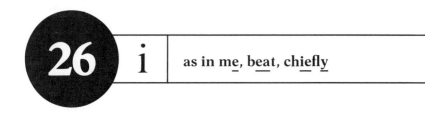

26   i | as in m<u>e</u>, b<u>ea</u>t, ch<u>ie</u>f<u>y</u>

I. PRONUNCIATION

To make this sound, raise the middle of your tongue high in the mouth and tense the muscles of your tongue and cheeks. Draw your lips back into a smile and make a voiced sound.

E	people	only
Ethiopia	thieves	maybe
eat	these	we
easy	teacher	be
either	meat	she
equal	read	me
evening	deep	three
even	seat	key

II. COMPARISON

Practice these contrasting sounds.

eat	it	feel	fill
seat	sit	leak	lick
feet	fit	sleep	slip
he'd	hid		

III. REPETITION

1. Please give me the key.
2. We are going to eat sandwiches and drink tea.
3. A breeze is blowing in from the east.

4. The meeting will be in three weeks.
5. Spell the word *badge*. B-a-d-g-e.
6. Even I had to agree that Steven was the obvious leader.
7. The sea air gave me renewed energy.
8. This evening we are completely booked; I'm sorry.

IV. PHRASING AND INTONATION

a. Blend together the words in each of these phrases to form a single unit—that is, pronounce each phrase as though it were a single word. Also stress the accented syllable strongly, obscuring the vowels in the remaining syllables

to tell a néighbor	on the ávenue	such a simple wáy
until the néxt time	climb an ápple tree	ordinary pláce
an easy lésson	plan to célebrate	Greek and Roman árt

b. The teacher reads each of the following sentences in a normal manner, giving some slight emphasis to phrasing and intonation. Students repeat after teacher. Teacher repeats after students.

1. (Teacher) Where is Peter working now?

   (Students) Where is Peter working now?
   (Teacher) Where is Peter working now?

2. (Teacher) He's working in a steel mill.

   (Students) He's working in a steel mill.
   (Teacher) He's working in a steel mill.

3. (Teacher) Do you feel well enough to go out?

   (Students) Do you feel well enough to go out?
   (Teacher) Do you feel well enough to go out?

Teacher and students continue in exactly the same manner with these sentences: Teacher reads, students repeat, teacher repeats.

4. I feel much better than I did last week.
5. Edith is reading over there by the peach tree.
6. Our teacher wants us to read some of Keats's poetry every day.
7. Sheila only works in the evening.
8. I don't believe that this report is complete.

V. CONTRACTIONS

In everyday speech, contracted verb forms are used more frequently than full forms. Practice these commonly used contractions:

Affirmative		*Negative*	
I am	I'm	is not	isn't
you are	you're	are not	aren't
he is	he's	was not	wasn't
she is	she's	were not	weren't
it is	it's	do not	don't
we are	we're	does not	doesn't
they are	they're	did not	didn't
I will	I'll	will not	won't
you will	you'll	have not	haven't
she will	she'll	has not	hasn't
etc.		can not	can't
I have	I've	could not	couldn't
you have	you've	should not	shouldn't
we have	we've	must not	mustn't
etc.		had not	hadn't
that is	that's	would not	wouldn't
there is	there's	need not	needn't
what is	what's		
I would	I'd		
you had	you'd		
they had	they'd		
we would	we'd		

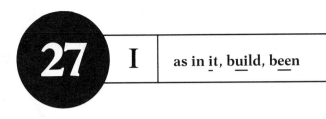

27 I as in it, build, been

I. PRONUNCIATION

To make this sound, raise your tongue high in your mouth; keep the muscles of your tongue, lips, and cheeks relaxed; and make a voiced sound.

fifty	Ms. [mɪz]	British
it	imagine	hill
if	Indian	kill
in	English	bit
ink	his	sit
into	ship	fill
is	rich	fit

II. COMPARISON

Practice these contrasting sounds.

still	steel		pill	peal
fill	feel		ship	sheep
hill	heel		bit	beat
lip	leap		sit	seat

III. REPETITION

1. His work has improved greatly since last year.
2. It gave him immense satisfaction to be able to compete with the others.

3. He has lived in all of the more interesting cities of the world.
4. The house is situated on the top of a hill.
5. On any clear day, the lake was easily visible in the distance.
6. There's only a little bit of milk left in the pitcher.
7. Their business made over a million dollars by April.
8. Jill's sister is still sick.

IV. PHRASING AND INTONATION

a. Blend together the words in each of these phrases or sentences to form a single unit—that is, pronounce each phrase as though it were a single word. Also stress the accented syllable rather strongly, obscuring the vowels in the remaining syllables accordingly.

two réindeer	six házelnuts	It's not for me to sáy.
a télex	not quíck enough	Whatever shall I dó?
We've béen there.	an émpty one	It's difficult to dó.

b. The teacher reads each of the following sentences in a normal manner, giving some slight emphasis to phrasing and intonation. Students repeat after teacher. Teacher repeats after students.

1. (Teacher)   Did you have that prescription filled?

     (Students)   Did you have that prescription filled?
     (Teacher)   Did you have that prescription filled?

2. (Teacher)   No, the doctor said I didn't need it.

     (Students)   No, the doctor said I didn't need it.
     (Teacher)   No, the doctor said I didn't need it.

3. (Teacher)   When did Bill leave for Chicago?

     (Students)   When did Bill leave for Chicago?
     (Teacher)   When did Bill leave for Chicago?

Teacher and students continue in exactly the same manner with these sentences: Teacher reads, students repeat, teacher repeats.

4. Is Mildred's sister still ill?
5. Yes, she has been ill for more than six weeks.
6. Where are Bill and Philip going?
7. I imagine that they're going fishing.
8. Is this ring yours?
9. No, that ring belongs to Isabel.
10. Those children drink a lot of milk.

V. PRONUNCIATION OF CONTRACTIONS

Practice these contracted verb forms, noting the distinction between those which are pronounced as one-syllable words and those which are pronounced as two-syllable words.

Pronounced as One Syllable		*Pronounced as Two Syllables*	
I'm	I've	isn't	I'll
you're	you've	wasn't	you'll
he's	we've	doesn't	she'll
she's	they've	didn't	he'll
it's	what's	haven't	it'll
we're	I'd	hadn't	we'll
they're	he'd	hasn't	they'll
aren't	we'd	couldn't	
weren't	won't	shouldn't	
don't		wouldn't	
can't		needn't	
that's		mustn't	
there's			
you'd			
she'd			
they'd			

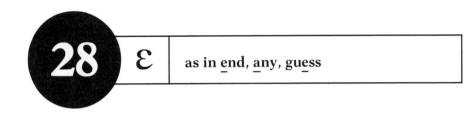

28 ɛ | as in <u>e</u>nd, <u>a</u>ny, g<u>ue</u>ss

I. PRONUNCIATION

To make this sound, draw back your lips, raise your tongue midway in your mouth, and make a short, voiced sound.

F	again	Wednesday
seven	dead	says
end	egg	set
any	edge	hen
else	envelope	beg
enter	get	men
excellent	dress	send

II. COMPARISON

Practice these contrasting sounds.

N	an	said	Sid
pen	pan	set	sit
end	and	well	will
beg	bag	dead	did
guess	gas	ten	tin
merry	marry	eminent	imminent

III. REPETITION

1. I didn't get up until twelve minutes after eleven this morning.
2. Helen was clever and intelligent.

3. He was a tall, slender, well-dressed man with elegant manners.
4. Betty will enter engineering school in February.
5. Ben sent a letter to his friend.
6. The fresh, gentle wind was welcome.
7. The entrance was hidden by a hedge which was ten feet tall.
8. In September, the Bensons are going to Venezuela.

IV. PHRASING AND INTONATION

a. Blend together the words in each of these phrases to form a single unit—that is, pronounce each phrase as though it were a single word. Also stress the accented syllable strongly, obscuring the vowels in the remaining syllables.

a glorious cóncert	an excellent foundátion	a good fríend
a well-written létter	a wonderful idéa	return sóon
What terrible wéather!	her annual vacátion	to stand úp

b. The teacher reads each of the following sentences in a normal manner, giving some slight emphasis to phrasing and intonation. Students repeat after teacher. Teacher repeats after students.

1. (Teacher) What else is there to tell?

   (Students) What else is there to tell?
   (Teacher) What else is there to tell?

2. (Teacher) We've given you every detail.

   (Students) We've given you every detail.
   (Teacher) We've given you every detail.

3. (Teacher) Can you lend Ted a pen?

   (Students) Can you lend Ted a pen?
   (Teacher) Can you lend Ted a pen?

Teacher and students continue in exactly the same manner with these sentences: Teacher reads, students repeat, teacher repeats.

4. There are several extra pens on my desk.
5. The entrance is at the end of the hall.
6. Have you read any good books lately?
7. The child rested his head on Edna's knee.
8. The leaves begin to turn color toward the end of September.

V. PRONUNCIATION OF CONTRACTIONS

Practice these contractions by repeating them along with their rhymes. *I'm* rhymes with *time* and *mime*.

you're: sure, pure
he's: please, sneeze
it's: sits, bits
we're: here, cheer
they're: care, fair
I'll: mile, pile
he'll: feel, deal
they'll: fail, male
I've: five, chive
we've: leave, grieve
they've: brave, save
that's: hats, spats
there's: cares, fares

you've: groove, move
you'll: cool, fool
weren't: burnt
we'll: feel, peal
can't: pant, chant
what's: ruts, nuts
I'd: hide, wide
you'd: rude, sued
she'd: need, read
they'd: paid, made

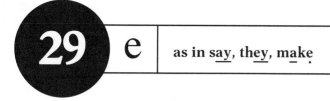

I. PRONUNCIATION

To make this sound, part your lips slightly, relax your tongue, and make a voiced sound just like the letter *a*.

A	maybe	neighbor
April	weight	vacation
age	baby	day
able	table	may
aim	paper	say
ache	date	stay
ate	same	they
eight	wait	away

II. COMPARISON

Practice these contrasting sounds.

lake	lack		late	let
mate	mat		main	men
fate	fat		gate	get
take	tack		date	debt

III. REPETITION

1. We'll wait for you in front of the main gate.
2. At this rate, we may complete the work later today.

3. The name of the song is "The Rain in Spain Stays Mainly in the Plain."
4. The account was paid in full on the stated date.
5. Jane is taking her paper to Ms. James.
6. They may stay here until April or May.
7. The lazy dog lay in the shade of the apple tree all day.
8. They may wait until a later date before making any decision.

IV. PHRASING AND INTONATION

a. Blend together the words in each of these phrases or sentences to form a single unit—that is, pronounce each phrase as though it were a single word. Also stress the accented syllable strongly, obscuring the vowels in the remaining syllables.

regret the dáy   blue skíes   stop the músic
They've gone awáy.   run drý   It's still ráining.
to bake a cáke   nice gúy   long-term stórage

b. The teacher reads each of the following sentences in a normal manner, giving some slight emphasis to phrasing and intonation. Students repeat after teacher. Teacher repeats after students.

1. (Teacher)   Can you stay and play another game?

   (Students) Can you stay and play another game?
   (Teacher)   Can you stay and play another game?

2. (Teacher)   I'm sorry — but it's getting late.

   (Students) I'm sorry — but it's getting late.
   (Teacher)   I'm sorry — but it's getting late.

3. (Teacher)   How much did they pay for the place?

   (Students) How much did they pay for the place?
   (Teacher)   How much did they pay for the place?

Teacher and students continue in exactly the same manner with these sentences: Teacher reads, students repeat, teacher repeats.

4. They paid over eighty thousand dollars.
5. Have you gained any weight lately?
6. Yes. On my vacation in Maine, I ate a lot.
7. How do you pronounce that name? I don't know, but you spell it K-h-a-j.
8. How long should we stay at the neighbor's party?

V. PRONUNCIATION OF THE *ea* VOWEL COMBINATION

This combination of letters may be pronounced in one of three different ways, each a single sound. Practice the vowel sounds in the following:

ea pronounced like the *e* in *see* [si]		*ea* pronounced like the *e* in *bed* [bɛd]		*ea* pronounced like the *a* in *take* [tek]
steal	leave	leather	pleasant	steak
please	meal	ready	instead	break
leaf	dream	bread	weather	great
weak	beach	health	already	
peace	speak	head	thread	
sea	cream	heaven	breakfast	
eagle	clean	dread	deaf	

30 æ | as in g<u>n</u>at, w<u>a</u>gon, la<u>u</u>gh

I. PRONUNCIATION

To make this short *a* sound, open your mouth, flatten your tongue, and make a voiced sound which is not nasal.

aunt	absent	man
apple	ran	example
angry	land	candy
at	laugh	wagon
action	matter	stamp
ask	catch	bag

II. COMPARISON

Practice these contrasting sounds.

bad	bed	hat	hot
sad	said	cat	cot
lad	led	map	mop
land	lend	cap	cop

III. REPETITION

1. The police officer ran after the man but did not catch him.
2. The black cat sat next to a large apple.
3. The accident happened shortly after our arrival.
4. Pat asked the man with the tan hat in his hand.
5. Harold sang a song and then performed a magic trick.

6. They began to speak Spanish.
7. Marion carried a bag and spoke a foreign language.
8. Grant plans to be back by January.

IV. PHRASING AND INTONATION

a. Blend together the words in each of these phrases or sentences to form a single unit—that is, pronounce each phrase as though it were a single word. Also stress the accented syllable strongly, obscuring the vowels in the remaining syllables.

hand in hánd	Use an ádjective.	What a handsome mán!
back and fórth	We ran áfter him.	Find a softer pád.
my last cláss	Give him áfter-shave.	Take a different stánd.

b. The teacher reads each of the following sentences in a normal manner, giving some slight emphasis to phrasing and intonation. Students repeat after teacher. Teacher repeats after students.

1. (Teacher)   Will Harry be|back soon?

   (Students)   Will Harry be back soon?
   (Teacher)   Will Harry be back soon?

2. (Teacher)   He plans to be back by|Saturday.

   (Students)   He plans to be back by Saturday.
   (Teacher)   He plans to be back by Saturday.

3. (Teacher)   When is your last|class?

   (Students)   When is your last class?
   (Teacher)   When is your last class?

Teacher and students continue in exactly the same manner with these sentences: Teacher reads, students repeat, teacher repeats.

4. My last class is at three o'clock in the afternoon.
5. Have you been asked to the dance on Saturday?
6. Yes, I'm going to the dance with Jack Brant.
7. Dan and Harry are having lunch in the cafeteria.
8. Jack failed to pass his mathematics examination.
9. She plans to spend the summer in France.
10. He who laughs last laughs best.

V. REVIEW DIALOGUE

- Good afternoon, madam. Our special for today is a ham sandwich with hot apple pie.
- Actually, I just came in for some coffee, but that apple pie sounds good. Perhaps I'll have a piece while I'm waiting.
- Is someone joining you, ma'am?
- My friend Anna Maria. She's happy today; she just got a job with Apple computers.
- They have a factory near here, don't they?
- Yes, and they're opening another in Catalina. That's where my friend will be working. Oh, there she is—the woman in the black skirt. You'd better make that two apple pies.

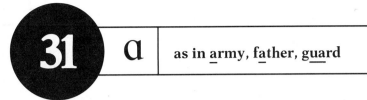

31 ɑ | as in <u>a</u>rmy, f<u>a</u>ther, g<u>ua</u>rd

I. PRONUNCIATION

To make this sound, open your mouth broadly, relax your tongue, and make a voiced, nonnasal sound like the exclamation "ahh!"

artist	honor	problem
architect	honest	not
arm	chocolate	far
art	garden	hot
are	politics	bomb
army	popular	Tom

II. COMPARISON

Practice these contrasting sounds, which are sometimes confused. Repeat several times.

not	nut		cot	cat
shot	shut		mop	map
cop	cup		hot	hat
fond	fund		cop	cap

III. REPETITION

1. A long line of palms stood as if guarding the entrance to the park.
2. The charges against Arthur were proven to be largely false.

3. The dog gave a sharp bark and then sprang at Tom.
4. Though a good driver, my father was never able to park the car well.
5. The argument started when the guard refused them entrance.
6. The architect is planning to start work on the garden next week.
7. Polly likes to go shopping during the holidays.
8. Dominic turned the doorknob the wrong way.

IV. PHRASING AND INTONATION

a. Blend together the words in each of these phrases or sentences to form a single unit—that is, pronounce each phrase as though it were a single word. Also stress the accented syllable strongly, obscuring the vowels in the remaining syllables.

an honest féllow	a rázor blade	Take a plane to Hóllywood.
tomorrow's dínner	a heárt attack	Tell me why it's bád for me.
a serious próblem	run ínto it	Throw away the Chrístmas tree.

b. The teacher reads each of the following sentences in a normal manner, giving some slight emphasis to phrasing and intonation. Students repeat after teacher. Teacher repeats after students.

1. (Teacher)   Where is your|father?

   (Students)   Where is your father?
   (Teacher)   Where is your father?

2. (Teacher)   He's in the barn with|Carl.

   (Students)   He's in the barn with Carl.
   (Teacher)   He's in the barn with Carl.

3. (Teacher)   Are you fond of modern|art?

(Students)   Are you fond of modern art?
(Teacher)   Are you fond of modern art?

Teacher and students continue in exactly the same manner with these sentences: Teacher reads, students repeat, teacher repeats.

4. Not particularly. Are you?
5. What are they arguing about so loudly?
6. They are arguing about politics—as usual.
7. Mr. and Mrs. Armstrong own a farm not far from town.
8. The lock on my car door does not work properly.

V. SILENT LETTERS

Practice these words, each of which contains one or more silent letters.

knife	build	answer
knee	scissors	doubt
handsome	calf	guard
honest	wrong	climb
knew	wrist	thumb
neighbor	listen	honor
knock	sword	walk
Wednesday	guilty	talk
kneel	whole	guest
scene	dumb	ghost
know	half	czar
guarantee	island	

32 ℐ as in h**er**, w**or**k, b**ir**d

I. PRONUNCIATION

To make this sound, tighten your cheek muscles and voice an "err" sound.

were	service	first
her	heard	bird
person	work	hurt
earn	word	curly
learn	worse	burn
earth	worst	turn

II. COMPARISON

Practice these contrasting sounds, which are sometimes confused. Repeat several times.

bird	Boyd	her	hair
verse	voice	were	wear
earl	oil	fur	fair
curl	coil	cur	care

III. REPETITION

1. We searched a long time for Pearl's purse.
2. The first and third verses were the most difficult to learn.
3. Earl has worked in that firm for many years.
4. It was early morning when we first heard the cries.

5. Though she worked hard, Gertrude earned little during the summer.
6. John's schoolwork seems to grow worse and worse.
7. Although her purse was returned, the contents were missing.
8. We have had no word from Earl since his return.

IV. PHRASING AND INTONATION

a. Blend together the words in each of these phrases or sentences to form a single unit—that is, pronounce each phrase as though it were a single word. Also stress the accented syllable rather strongly, obscuring the vowels in the remaining syllables accordingly.

What a pretty bírd!   He learns quíckly.   dangerous medicátion
to be out of wórk   frigid wáter   prosperous habitátion
He has curly háir.   They were búsy.   a tall and skinny
                                                                      player

b. The teacher reads each of the following sentences in a normal manner, giving some slight emphasis to phrasing and intonation. Students repeat after teacher. Teacher repeats after students.

1. (Teacher)   How did Gertrude hurt her hand?

   (Students) How did Gertrude hurt her hand?
   (Teacher)   How did Gertrude hurt her hand?

2. (Teacher)   She hurt it while working in the kitchen.

   (Students) She hurt it while working in the kitchen.
   (Teacher)   She hurt it while working in the kitchen.

3. (Teacher)   Are both girls learning German?

   (Students) Are both girls learning German?
   (Teacher)   Are both girls learning German?

Teacher and students continue in exactly the same manner with these sentences: Teacher reads, students repeat, teacher repeats.

4. Yes, both girls are studying German at the university.
5. Why is Ernest leaving home so early?
6. He's working nights, trying to earn some extra money.
7. While stepping off the curb, Earl turned his ankle.
8. Bert served three terms in the foreign service.
9. The first and third words were difficult to pronounce.
10. Mr. Burns hopes to return early next week.

V. REVIEW DIALOGUE

- Are you worried about the concert tonight? Herbert says he thinks your last rehearsal was terrible.
- He's right. We were all off-key in the first and third verses.
- He says there is even one person who hasn't learned all the words yet.
- That's Bernadette Burns. She hurries through the choruses, and it hurts the rest of us.
- Perhaps you should go to the hall early tonight to rehearse some more. It can't hurt; and, according to Herbert, you can't get any worse.
- We were going to work late today, but I think you're right, sir. We'd better practice.

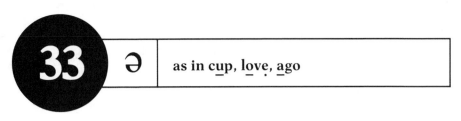

33 ə | as in c<u>u</u>p, l<u>o</u>ve, <u>a</u>go

I. PRONUNCIATION

To make this sound, open your mouth slightly, relax your tongue, and make a short, voiced sound.

us	love	trouble
up	come	enough
under	some	country
much	son	soda
cut	done	mama

II. COMPARISON

Practice these contrasting sounds.

fun	fan	cut	caught
run	ran	but	bought
mud	mad	done	dawn
rug	rag	gun	gone

III. REPETITION

1. We were unable to reach you on Sunday or Monday.
2. My mother was upset when she heard of my uncle's accident.
3. Something must be done at once!
4. Come again tomorrow for another cup of coffee.
5. My cousin and I often hunt in the country.

6. The people under us are noisy, but the people above us are wonderfully quiet.
7. The judge cut short the trial and had the prisoner hustled from the courtroom.
8. The umpire looked funny holding an umbrella.

IV. PHRASING AND INTONATION

a. Blend together the words in each of these phrases or sentences to form a single unit—that is, pronounce each phrase as though it were a single word. Also stress the accented syllable strongly, obscuring the vowels in the remaining syllables.

a cup of cóffee	a shóe store	a múd puddle
She cut her fínger.	a tíme bomb	a téa kettle
a funny stóry	too lázy	a stéam engine

b. The teacher reads each of the following sentences in a normal manner, giving some slight emphasis to phrasing and intonation. Students repeat after teacher. Teacher repeats after students.

1. (Teacher) Do you have any money with you?

   (Students) Do you have any money with you?
   (Teacher) Do you have any money with you?

2. (Teacher) I have some but not very much.

   (Students) I have some but not very much.
   (Teacher) I have some but not very much.

3. (Teacher) What different subjects did he cover?

   (Students) What different subjects did he cover?
   (Teacher) What different subjects did he cover?

Teacher and students continue in exactly the same manner with these sentences: Teacher reads, students repeat, teacher repeats.

4. He dealt with some suggestions concerning the construction of a new subway.
5. Do you want to come to the country with us to do some hunting?
6. I'd love to, but this report must be done by one o'clock.
7. The old woman gave her age as "one hundred years young."
8. Two months ago, my mother and brother got into trouble.

V. STRESS: STRONG AND WEAK FORMS

English words of more than one syllable are strongly accented on one syllable. The remaining syllables receive less stress. Unstressed syllables are usually pronounced [ə]. The same is true for one-syllable words that are in unstressed positions in a phrase or sentence.

Practice these one-syllable words in both their strong forms and their weak forms (in the unstressed positions of the phrase or sentence).

Word	Strong Form	Weak Form Used in Normal Speech	
a	[e]	[ə]	a big bóy
an	[æn]	[ən]	Eat an ápple.
and	[ænd]	[ənd]	you and Í
the	[ði]	[ðə]	on the wáy
are	[ɑr]	[ər]	They are búsy.
to	[tu]	[tə]	Go to schóol.
can	[kæn]	[kən]	She can wáit.
have	[hæv]	[həv]	They have léft.
has	[hæz]	[həz]	He has góne.
had	[hæd]	[həd]	We had séen it.
that	[ðæt]	[ðət]	the one that cáme

34 u | **as in too, shoe, fruit**

I. PRONUNCIATION

To make this sound, round your lips, raise your tongue midway in the mouth, and make a long, voiced sound.

U	June	juice
rule	soup	grew
soon	group	crew
tooth	move	chew
movie	room	blew
food	true	flew
school	blue	through

II. COMPARISON

Practice these contrasting sounds.

soon	sun	shoe	show
shoot	shut	crew	crow
room	rum	soup	soap
school	skull	noon	known

III. REPETITION

1. We were in no mood to go swimming in the pool.
2. The crew could do nothing against the strong wind, which blew from the south.

3. The cool weather caused the flowers to droop and to lose their bright colors.
4. The fact that it would soon be June and there would be no more school pleased all of us.
5. We had a choice of soup or fruit juice for the first course.
6. They are moving to New Mexico in June.
7. Ruth is leaving at noon for New York.
8. It was stupid of him to refuse such a good opportunity.

IV. PHRASING AND INTONATION

a. Blend together the words in each of these phrases or sentences to form a single unit—that is, pronounce each phrase as though it were a single word. Also stress the accented syllable strongly, obscuring the vowels in the remaining syllables.

Use a táblespoon.	What a beautiful dáy!	thanks to the
take a pleásure	He's a generous mán.	hóneybee
trip	Take a tip from a	change for a
Uncle Geórge	friénd.	bétter one
was here.		harder to éducate

b. The teacher reads each of the following sentences in a normal manner, giving some slight emphasis to phrasing and intonation. Students repeat after teacher. Teacher repeats after students.

1. (Teacher)   What's the matter with Sue?

   (Students) What's the matter with Sue?
   (Teacher)   What's the matter with Sue?

2. (Teacher)   She has a bad toothache.

   (Students) She has a bad toothache.
   (Teacher)   She has a bad toothache.

3. (Teacher)   Is your group going to the zoo today?

(Students)   Is your group going to the zoo today?
(Students)   Is your group going to the zoo today?

Teacher and students continue in exactly the same manner with these sentences: Teacher reads, students repeat, teacher repeats.

4.   Yes, we're planning to leave around noon.
5.   Is it too soon to call Stuart?
6.   Lulu said she was moving to New York soon.
7.   Whom did they choose at the meeting this afternoon?
8.   I think I'll wear my blue shoes today.

V. HOMONYMS

Practice these pairs of homonyms and distinguish their meanings.

hear	here	know	no
seem	seam	pear	pare
some	sum	plane	plain
hole	whole	piece	peace
higher	hire	buy	by
him	hymn	role	roll
meet	meat	guessed	guest
made	maid	steal	steel
mail	male	so	sew
in	inn	son	sun
berry	bury	principle	principal
our	hour	dear	deer
break	brake	one	won

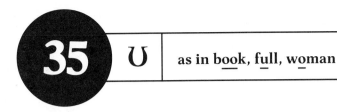

35 Ʊ | **as in b<u>oo</u>k, f<u>u</u>ll, w<u>o</u>man**

I. PRONUNCIATION

To make this sound, push your lips out slightly, raise your tongue midway in your mouth, and make a short, voiced sound.

good	look	butcher
wood	stood	woolen
would	sugar	push
pull	woman	put
took	bullet	cushion
cook	could	bushel

II. COMPARISON

Practice these contrasting sounds.

brook	broke		pull	pool
pull	pole		full	fool
bull	bowl		stood	stewed
could	code		look	Luke

III. REPETITION

1. Was the movie *Tootsie* as good as the one you took me to?
2. The woman wore a good-looking wool jacket.
3. We should put some more wood on the fire.
4. This cookbook says to put more sugar in the pudding.
5. She stood when she should have sat.

6. I took the blanket and shook it before putting it over us.
7. It looks as though Ms. Goodman's pool is full.
8. The butcher put a cushion on his chair.

IV. PHRASING AND INTONATION

a. Blend together the words in each of these phrases to form a single unit—that is, pronounce each phrase as though it were a single word. Also stress the accented syllable strongly, obscuring the vowels in the remaining syllables.

a good boók	run the race to wín	a wool sweáter
a full moón	at the proper tíme	deny nóthing
I'm not súre.	help the man to swím	until aútumn

b. The teacher reads each of the following sentences in a normal manner, giving some slight emphasis to phrasing and intonation. Students repeat after teacher. Teacher repeats after students.

1. (Teacher)   Is John a good student?

   (Students)   Is John a good student?
   (Teacher)   Is John a good student?

2. (Teacher)   He would be a good student if he studied more.

   (Students)   He would be a good student if he studied more.
   (Teacher)   He would be a good student if he studied more.

3. (Teacher)   In which part of Brooklyn do they live?

   (Students)   In which part of Brooklyn do they live?
   (Teacher)   In which part of Brooklyn do they live?

Teacher and students continue in exactly the same manner with these sentences: Teacher reads, students repeat, teacher repeats.

4. There is nothing I'd rather do than read a good book.
5. She stood at the woodpile and asked if she could help.
6. This woman's coat comes with a hood attached.
7. We all felt sure that she would get sick.
8. We pushed and pulled, but we could not open the door.
9. From which cookbook did you get this recipe?
10. Mr. Brooks's hand shook as he signed the contract.

V. REVIEW DIALOGUE

- Hello, Wood residence.
- Hi, I'm responding to your ad in the paper, the one that says, "Cabin in the woods for rent."
- This is the place. It's called Brookhaven because there's a brook running near the cabin. There's a good wood-burning stove in the kitchen and a fireplace in the living room. It's quite a cozy nook.
- I see. What would we need to bring with us?
- Only the food you want to cook. Everything else is already there. You should dress warmly. It's cold this time of year. Bring wool sweaters if you have them.
- I'm looking forward to getting away to a place where I can read some good books in peace.
- Brookhaven is just the place for you, then. I could send you some more information in the mail, if you'd like.

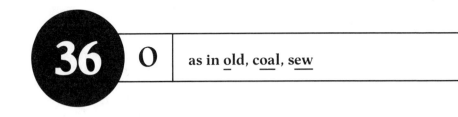

36 | O | **as in <u>o</u>ld, c<u>oa</u>l, s<u>ew</u>**

I. PRONUNCIATION

To make this sound, round your lips and make a long "oh" sound.

O	phone	though
Ohio	Joe	no
ocean	don't	go
over	wrote	show
open	those	so
only	home	low
obey	both	snow
omit		

II. COMPARISON

Practice these contrasting sounds.

note	nut		loan	lawn
home	hum		boat	bought
phone	fun		coat	caught
known	none		low	law

III. REPETITION

1. Joan rolled over and over on the lawn.
2. She won't only give her opinion; she'll give both their opinions.
3. No notice was given of the closing of the show.

4. He wore an old coat that no one else would have dared to put on.
5. No one knows where or when he obtained the loan.
6. Mr. and Mrs. Joseph are leaving for Rome in November.
7. You should fold your clothes more carefully before packing them.
8. For a moment, Joe did not know whether to laugh or cry.

IV. PHRASING AND INTONATION

a. Blend together the words in each of these phrases or sentences to form a single unit—that is, pronounce each phrase as though it were a single word. Also stress the accented syllable strongly, obscuring the vowels in the remaining syllables.

The window's ópen.	a tréndsetter	gó for it
Tell that to Jósie.	The phóne's ringing.	síng to her
a single páper	the stóck market	fínger paint

b. The teacher reads each of the following sentences in a normal manner, giving some slight emphasis to phrasing and intonation. Students repeat after teacher. Teacher repeats after students.

1. (Teacher)   Did you enjoy the show?

   (Students)   Did you enjoy the show?
   (Teacher)   Did you enjoy the show?

2. (Teacher)   Although the author is well known,

                 the play was not so good.

   (Students)   Although the author is well known,
                     the play was not so good.
   (Teacher)   Although the author is well known,
                     the play was not so good.

3. (Teacher)   Who is the author of that|poem?

(Students) Who is the author of that poem?
(Teacher)   Who is the author of that poem?

Teacher and students continue in exactly the same manner with these sentences: Teacher reads, students repeat, teacher repeats.

4. Joe voted for Homer Bolton.
5. She wrote it in November.
6. I rowed in a lake in Oklahoma.
7. We go to North Dakota, but not too often.
8. I don't know how old Josephine is.
9. Don't open the window; it's too cold.
10. Most of my clothes are old.

V. PRONUNCIATION OF THE *ou* VOWEL COMBINATION

This combination of letters may be pronounced in several different ways, each a single sound. Practice the vowel sounds in the following:

ou pronounced like the *o* in *over* [óvɚ]	*ou* pronounced like the *u* in *but* [bət]	*ou* pronounced like the *ow* in *how* [haʊ]
dough	cousin	loud
shoulder	rough	sound
soul	enough	out
though	couple	cloud
cantaloupe	double	proud
boulder	country	south
doughnut	trouble	found
although	tough	amount
		around
		house
		about

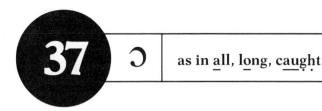

37 ɔ | as in <u>a</u>ll, l<u>o</u>ng, c<u>au</u>ght

I. PRONUNCIATION

To make this sound, place your tongue in a low, mid-back position, tense your lips, and push them forward.

coffee	awful	gone
almost	author	fought
fall	although	bought
walk	always	draw
small	also	taught
law	salt	saw
autumn	hall	cough

II. COMPARISON

Practice these contrasting sounds.

walk	woke	ball	bowl	hall	hole
law	low	paw	pow	lost	lust
bought	boat	gnaw	now	boss	bus
call	coal	saw	sow	long	lung

III. REPETITION

1. A large audience listened to the auctioneer.
2. We saw a shawl lying in the hallway.
3. Paul has a bad cough, which he caught while swimming.

4. We altered our plans and decided to walk rather than to go by automobile.
5. It was obvious to all that the law must be withdrawn.
6. In his audit of the books, the auditor caught many errors.
7. Pauline bought a new fall coat this year.
8. The dog walked in the water we were going to use to make coffee.

IV. PHRASING AND INTONATION

a. Blend together the words in each of these phrases or sentences to form a single unit—that is, pronounce each phrase as though it were a single word. Also stress the accented syllable strongly, obscuring the vowels in the remaining syllables.

find new lánds to explore	a páwnshop	What's néw about it, Sam?
a new phóto for you	políce car	It's trúe that it's a fake.
to fall óver something	addréss book	Stand stíll for heaven's sake.

b. The teacher reads each of the following sentences in a normal manner, giving some slight emphasis to phrasing and intonation. Students repeat after teacher. Teacher repeats after students.

1. (Teacher)   Where is Shawn's daughter?

   (Students)   Where is Shawn's daughter?
   (Teacher)   Where is Shawn's daughter?

2. (Teacher)   She's walking to Windom Hall.

   (Students)   She's walking to Windom Hall.
   (Teacher)   She's walking to Windom Hall.

3. (Teacher)   Have you ever been abroad?

(Students)   Have you ever been abroad?
(Teacher)   Have you ever been abroad?

  Teacher and students continue in exactly the same manner with these sentences: Teacher reads, students repeat, teacher repeats.

4. I spent a few weeks in Austria last autumn.
5. Who is the author of that story?
6. The story was written by Nathaniel Hawthorne.
7. Who is going to teach that course during August?
8. Miss Ball taught it last August.
9. Paul should not talk that way about Walter.
10. The Music Hall always draws a large audience.

V. REVIEW DIALOGUE

- Have you ever been to an auction before?
- No, this is my first. I feel awkward. This place looks like a cross between a pawnshop and an antique hall in a museum. Oh, look! There's the auctioneer.
- He's going to offer an old Spanish shawl first. Let's pass on that and go over to inspect those straw items. I love straw!
- This auburn-haired Australian doll looks interesting, but it's awfully expensive.
- Listen. People are applauding; I wonder if the auction is all over.
- I doubt it. People often applaud when an item sells well. Let's walk this way. I think I caught a glimpse of a small water pitcher I'd like to bid for.
- I thought you'd get around to bidding before the day was over.

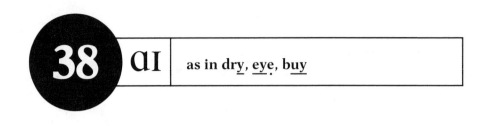

38 aɪ | as in dr**y**, e**ye**, b**uy**

I. PRONUNCIATION

To make this sound, combine the sound [ɑ] as in *father* with the sound [ɪ] as in *city*. This diphthong produces the long *i* sound.

I	time	by
eye	night	my
ice	like	sigh
aisle	dime	lie
idea	quite	die
island	quiet	pie

II. COMPARISON

Practice these contrasting sounds.

tie	toy	time	team
aisle	oil	mine	mean
buy	boy	by	be
tile	toil	pie	pea

III. REPETITION

1. The island is isolated and difficult to reach—especially at night.
2. His poor eyesight made it useless for him to try for the prize.
3. Each item you buy is itemized on the monthly bill.

4. Mr. Wright was so frightened that he dropped both knife and rifle and ran away.
5. Ira is a fine fellow with very high ideals.
6. Irene and Ida sat side by side throughout the entire meeting.
7. This Friday is the ninth of July.
8. As soon as I said "Hi," he said "Good-bye."

IV. PHRASING AND INTONATION

a. Blend together the words in each of these phrases or sentences to form a single unit—that is, pronounce each phrase as though it were a single word. Also stress the accented syllable strongly, obscuring the vowels in the remaining syllables

a fine níght	What tíme is it?	a knife and a fórk
a bright bóy	Unwráp the thing.	the scene of the críme
to turn ríght	Give ín to him.	to sit side by síde

b. The teacher reads each of the following sentences in a normal manner, giving some slight emphasis to phrasing and intonation. Students repeat after teacher. Teacher repeats after students.

1. (Teacher) What kind of ice|cream|shall I buy?

   (Students) What kind of ice cream shall I buy?
   (Teacher) What kind of ice cream shall I buy?

2. (Teacher) Vanilla goes well with apple|pie.

   (Students) Vanilla goes well with apple pie.
   (Teacher) Vanilla goes well with apple pie.

3. (Teacher) Is Irene|younger than her sister?

   (Students) Is Irene younger than her sister?
   (Teacher) Is Irene younger than her sister?

Teacher and students continue in exactly the same manner with these sentences: Teacher reads, students repeat, teacher repeats.

4. Yes, but she's older than her brother Mike.
5. What time is it, please?
6. It's exactly five o'clock by my watch.
7. It's a lovely night. Let's go for a ride somewhere.
8. How about driving to Long Island?

V. PRONUNCIATION OF VOWELS AND FINAL VOICED CONSONANTS

When any vowel in English precedes a final voiced consonant, it is held longer than when it precedes a final unvoiced consonant. The vowel[æ] in the word *bag,* for example, is held slightly longer than the same vowel in *back.* The vowel [ɪ] in *pig* is held longer than the same vowel in *pick.*

Practice these vowel and consonant sounds:

Final Consonant Voiced	*Final Consonant Unvoiced*
bag	back
pig	pick
tag	tack
heard	hurt
need	neat
add	at
had	hat
ride	right
rode	wrote
spend	spent
build	built
said	set
lend	lent

39 | aʊ | as in c<u>ow</u>, <u>our</u>, h<u>ou</u>s<u>e</u>.

I. PRONUNCIATION

To make this sound, combine the sound [ɑ] as in *father* with the sound [ʊ] as in *book*.

our	about	how
hour	around	cow
ourselves	down	now
out	house	town
outside	found	allow

II. COMPARISON

Practice these contrasting sounds.

town	ton	now	no	cows	cause
found	fun	loud	load	down	dawn
down	done	found	phoned	loud	laud
shout	shut	town	tone	louse	loss

III. REPETITION

1. Howard was not allowed to go out of the house.
2. Our house is around the corner from the town hall.
3. No one knows how the mouse got into the house.
4. They spend hours in their flower garden.
5. The cow weighed about a thousand pounds.
6. The dark clouds seem to be coming from the south.

7. *Hour* is a noun, but *our* is not.
8. I doubt that Mr. Brown knows how to make that sound.

IV. PHRASING AND INTONATION

a. Blend together the words in each of these phrases or sentences to form a single unit—that is, pronounce each phrase as though it were a single word. Also stress the accented syllable strongly, obscuring the vowels in the remaining syllables.

to buy a hoúse	to find oút	all the fine young
We caught a moúse.	now and thén	sóldiers
to play outsíde	north and soúth	Tell me all the stóries.
		chimps and apes and
		mónkeys

b. The teacher reads each of the following sentences in a normal manner, giving some slight emphasis to phrasing and intonation. Students repeat after teacher. Teacher repeats after students.

1. (Teacher) How much time should I allow to go downtown?

   (Students) How much time should I allow to go downtown?
   (Teacher) How much time should I allow to go downtown?

2. (Teacher) It will take you at least an hour.

   (Students) It will take you at least an hour.
   (Teacher) It will take you at least an hour.

3. (Teacher) Is Mrs. Brown a good housekeeper?

   (Students) Is Mrs. Brown a good housekeeper?
   (Teacher) Is Mrs. Brown a good housekeeper?

Teacher and students continue in exactly the same manner with these sentences: Teacher reads, students repeat, teacher repeats.

4. Why is the crowd shouting so wildly?
5. The proud author took another bow.
6. How did Howie cut his eyebrow?
7. I once found an eight-ounce mushroom.
8. Their house is down that street.

V. THE FINAL *e*

When *e* is the final letter of an English word, it is usually not pronounced (particularly when it comes after a consonant). This final *e* does, however, affect the pronunciation of the word.

Practice pronouncing these pairs of words, and distinguish between their meanings:

car	care	rid	ride
far	fare	plan	plane
bar	bare	shin	shine\
win	wine	hat	hate
cap	cape	pan	pane
cloth	clothe	can	cane
breath	breathe	pin	pine
dim	dime	at	ate
rat	rate	pal	pale
star	stare	not	note
fat	fate	quit	quite
ton	tone	spin	spine

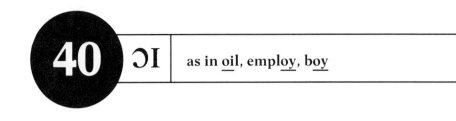

40 **ɔI** | **as in <u>oi</u>l, empl<u>oy</u>, b<u>oy</u>**

I. PRONUNCIATION

To make this sound, combine the sound of [ɔ] as in *pawn* with the sound of [ɪ] as in *city*.

boil	broil	voice
soil	poison	choice
coin	voyage	destroy
oyster	appoint	noisy
spoil	noise	boy
royal	point	employ

II. COMPARISON

Practice these contrasting sounds.

oil	earl	boil	ball	voice	vice
coil	curl	coil	call	oil	I'll
voice	verse	oil	all	toy	tile
oily	early	toil	tall	poise	pies

III. REPETITION

1. The smell of oil annoyed us.
2. The boys' voices added to the noise
3. Sigmund Freud enjoyed a meal of oysters.
4. Boyd is employed at a toy store.
5. During our voyage, we studied the royal families of Europe.

6. We had no choice but to send them another invoice.
7. Joyce and Floyd are playing a game of quoits.
8. Roy voided his ticket to Detroit and went to Troy instead.

IV. PHRASING AND INTONATION

a. Blend together the words in each of these phrases to form a single unit—that is, pronounce each phrase as though it were a single word. Also stress the accented syllable strongly, obscuring the vowels in the remaining syllables.

a long vóyage	remaining érror	soft líghts
the boys' vóices	delightful stóry	full móon
a sad énding	exciting móment	not yét

b. The teacher reads each of the following sentences in a normal manner, giving some slight emphasis to phrasing and intonation. Students repeat after teacher. Teacher repeats after students.

1. (Teacher)   Did you enjoy your voyage to Europe?

   (Students) Did you enjoy your voyage to Europe?
   (Teacher)   Did you enjoy your voyage to Europe?

2. (Teacher)   We enjoyed it very much, thank you.

   (Students) We enjoyed it very much, thank you.
   (Teacher)   We enjoyed it very much, thank you.

3. (Teacher)   When did Floyd join your club?

   (Students) When did Floyd join your club?
   (Teacher)   When did Floyd join your club?

Teacher and students continue in exactly the same manner with these sentences: Teacher reads, students repeat, teacher repeats.

4. He joined shortly after his appointment as treasurer.
5. I see no point in avoiding them any longer.
6. Personally, I don't like oysters in any form: raw, boiled, or broiled.
7. Roy really spoiled the party by being so noisy all afternoon.
8. His choice was a selection from James Joyce.

V. A RULE OF ACCENT

The opposites of many words in English are formed by the addition of various prefixes. A secondary accent in the word containing such a prefix generally falls on this prefix.

Practice these words noting primary (´) and secondary (`) stresses.

attráctive	ùnattráctive	fáir	ùnfáir
advántage	dìsadvántage	convénient	ìnconvénient
fórtunate	ùnfórtunate	agréeable	dìsagréeable
políte	ìmpolíte	pronoúnce	mìspronoúnce
corréct	ìncorréct	connéct	dìsconnéct
fúrnished	ùnfúrnished	contínue	dìscontínue
kínd	ùnkínd	understánd	mìsunderstánd
sátisfied	dìssátisfied	bútton	ùnbútton
pleásant	ùnpleásant	agrée	dìsagrée
depéndent	ìndepéndent	appróve	dìsappróve
belíevable	ùnbelíevable	obéy	dìsobéy
háppy	ùnháppy	inhérit	dìsinhérit